BISMARCK
and
Modern Germany

D1376415

BISMARCK
and
Modern Germany

BY

W. N. MEDLICOTT

Perennial Library
Harper & Row, Publishers, New York

Contents

CONTENTS

Preface

IN writing this little book the point that has perhaps interested me most has been the contrast between the earlier and later stages of Bismarck's public life, and I have tried to find some explanation of the psychological issues which in part underlie it. The general aim, however, has been to give a brief survey of Bismarck's whole career, in the light of the more critical estimates of his work which have appeared in Germany since 1945 (they have always been abundant abroad, although he has had his admirers there too). Owing to conditions of space I have made no serious attempt to refer to the views of the many writers who have preceded me, and whose judgments I am tending to accept or to controvert at every stage. Nor does the short bibliography represent anything like the full list of works which I have found illuminating and useful; although it does exclude any that I have not. I hope, however, that it will be sufficient for anyone wishing to embark on a serious study of this extraordinary and many-sided man.

W. N. M.

Chapter One

Young Bismarck and Old Prussia

OTTO EDUARD LEOPOLD VON BISMARCK, the second surviving son of a Junker squire, was born at the family home of Schönhausen in Brandenburg, some sixty miles to the west of Berlin, on 1 April 1815. His ancestors, whose family tree stretched back to the days of Charlemagne, had served the Hohenzollern rulers of Brandenburg-Prussia with unfailing loyalty and unswerving mediocrity since the sixteenth century. We are on safe ground in assuming that Otto derived his intelligence from his mother. Wilhelmine Mencken was the daughter of a distinguished official of middle-class stock in the service of Frederick the Great and his successor, and it was she, and not her husband, who directed her son's schooling and even found him some friends at court. For this he seems to have felt little gratitude, and he grew into a large and splendid but decidedly dissatisfied young man, restless like many others amid the stagnant politics of post-Napoleonic Germany.

His mother's plan for the young man was a good steady career in the Prussian civil service. The alternatives were to become either an officer in the army or a farmer on his own estates. He accepted the first suggestion, hoping for a diplomatic career. In preparation for the examination he spent three semesters at the University of Göttingen in Hanover (still ruled by the King of England), and three at Berlin, when his debts made it convenient for him to work at home. He had a phase of membership in the *Burschenschaften*, students' societies devoted to the cherishing of the revolutionary spirit; as the members were destined for the most part to become respectable bureaucrats their liberal wild oats were of no great consequence, but Bismarck tells us that he disliked their manners. He found the membership of an aristocratic students-corps, the Hanovera, more congenial, and there followed much drinking, duelling (with many successes), love affairs, cutting of lectures, and all the typical and no doubt delightful wild life of the favoured German adolescent of the period.

In 1835 he began a short and undistinguished career as a civil servant (*Auskultator*) mainly at Aix-la-Chappelle (Aachen). Here he spent much of his spare time with the international set of the town, and there were reports of gambling and dissipation; he finally fell in love with an English girl who jilted him in favour of a one-armed colonel with a fortune. In pursuing her he evidently neglected his official duties. He served his year of compulsory military service at Potsdam, which brought him further contacts with the court, but early in 1839 he was led by debts, boredom with the civil service, and his mother's death to retire to the family estate of Kniephof, where he had spent his early years. Working with his elder brother he succeeded in putting the property into better financial condition, but in spite of some sentimental professions the return to the soil did not satisfy him, and there were many reports of the wild life of the mad (and obviously bored) Junker of Kniephof. He continued to travel when he could afford it, to England and elsewhere.

All this corresponds pretty closely to Bismarck's own later accounts of his early life, in which no doubt there were some romantic touches, for like many famous men he seems to have enjoyed stories about his own wild youth. But he also found time for wide reading, much of it in history and foreign literature, including Shakespeare; he had learned to speak French and English well, and he had made useful and interesting friends, including Albrecht von Roon. The wildness was not necessarily typical of the youth of the times. There were tensions and contradictions in his character which were personal to himself and which for want of a better explanation are usually attributed to the contrasting qualities of his parents. From his extremely undistinguished and improvident father he presumably inherited his large frame, his strength, appetites, rough humour, liking for the country; from his mother he inherited sensitivity, sharp wits, and capacity for boredom with country life. But the contrast may be too abrupt. The difficulty of making much headway in anything that he undertook in his earlier years did not lessen his arrogant confidence in his own will power and genius, and when he entered politics these in turn were not diminished by his contemplation of the unprofitable moderation and inelastic conservatism of the Prussian politicians of the day. A sense of frustration and an opportunity to satisfy it in politics went together.

Two streams of aspiration were giving some direction to the more active and restless minds in Prussian society. The heritage of the Goethe period was precious if only because it proved that there were souls capable of culture, receptive of the best in cosmopolitan society, and able to foster the young growth of national feeling in a liberal atmosphere. On the other hand the cult of efficiency and loyalty with which Frederick the Great and his father had endowed the state had no place for liberal romanticism, was unconcerned with culture, but offered the triumph of disciplined power.

Could liberal culture and Prussian discipline be combined? Was the military spirit capable of exercising power? Must the man of ideas and ambition make his choice, or could he swim in both streams, the enlightened servant of a disciplined establishment? Bismarck as a young man had not achieved this synthesis, but he had not yet made the choice. The partial escape from Junkerdom represented by his mother's influence, his wide reading and travels, together with phases of scepticism, political liberalism, and cosmopolitan friendship, had not been entirely renounced on his return to Kniephof. In his first incursion into the political battles after 1847 his instinct for an effective role led him to defend the conservative position uncompromisingly, and his ideas did not seem to go beyond the maintenance of the rights of the dynasty, the Junkers, and the Prussian state as it shuddered under the impact of the 1848 revolution. And yet this upsurge of dynastic loyalty did not entirely drive from his mind the merits, or at least the usefulness, of the other Germany.

It was evident, however, to him and his friends that Prussia's position in German politics did not make possible at the moment anything more than a grim defence of her existing position. She was accepted by Austria and Russia as a major power, and was associated with them in a conservative attitude towards the international problems of the day. But it was a somewhat patronizing relationship on their part. She had emerged from the Napoleonic struggle with three main handicaps. Her population was only a third of that of France or Austria; her ruler, King Frederick William III, was unwilling for adventures, particularly if they meant trouble with the Austrians; and she was generally unpopular in the other German states. In the 18th century Frederick the Great's luck, personality, and military ability had raised his poor and well-drilled country to a position which his successors could not sustain. Her military reputation was destroyed by Napoleon at Jena in 1806. Her reforming ministers, Stein and Hardenberg, had introduced reforms after 1807 which included the emancipation of the serfs and various concessions to commoners, but this was not so much a liberal revolution as an attempt to win support for the government in the final struggle with the French. The country was still mainly rural, the middle class were small and weak, the peasantry in the Junker-dominated areas were loyal to the King and to their landlords. The nobility remained dominant in the army and local government. Change would probably be for the worse, and it seemed best to avoid trouble.

This rigid, militaristic, self-contained Prussianism was sometimes known as Borussism (*Borussismus*), and it was continually being challenged by developments elsewhere in the state. One of the strangest features of the peace settlement had been Prussia's advance to the Rhine. While Austria had no desire to strengthen a rival she had found it convenient in 1815 to give up her older dominions in the Rhineland and southern Netherlands in order to consolidate her Italian and Slavonic possessions. Prussia had been forced by the Tsar in 1815 to abandon most of her designs on Polish territory, but she received in compensation two-thirds of Saxony and large territories in west and north-western Germany, where a mass of smaller states and principalities were combined into the two new provinces of Rhineland and Westphalia under her rule. Thus her population was more than doubled; and she had been given, with Talleyrand's surprising approval, the military role of defending the western frontier against a future French attack. But as most of her acquisitions had been at the expense of other German states she was feared and disliked. The Prussian bureaucracy, carrying out a necessary task of administrative consolidation with earnest efficiency, increased the profound psychological cleavage between the rather francophil Rhinelanders and Saxons, and the stiff-necked and reputedly uncultured Prussians. Did not a censor in the Rhineland, who was destined to have many tussles with Karl Marx, suppress an advertisement for a translation of Dante's *Divine Comedy* on the ground that no comedy should be made of divine things?

Bismarck would have had personal knowledge of the unpopularity of his colleagues at Aachen if he had not been so tied up with the cosmopolitan social life of the town. But he knew enough to realize that these extensive commitments did not carry a corresponding assertion of strength. The surviving thirty-eight German states had been combined in 1815 into the German Confederation, and the smaller states tended to look to Austria, the presiding power, as their defender against Prussian pretensions. It is true, however, that from 1819 onwards one state after another had found it useful or expedient to join the customs union planned by the Prussian Ministry of Finance, and the whole group was joined in the *Deutscher Zollverein* in March 1833. This included four-fifths of the states that made up the German empire in 1871; it gave Germany a large measure of economic unity a generation before political union was achieved; and it left out Austria.

There were therefore some curious contradictions and potential advantages in Prussia's situation. The smaller states might look to Austria for support against Prussia, but they might have to look to Prussia for support against France and for their economic survival. For the time being, however, the governments of all the states (including Austria and Prussia) were in varying degrees conservative and torpid and apprehensive, none quite sure of its security after the Napoleonic shake-up, none quite able to trust its neighbours. Liberal and nationalist enthusiasts, a growing class after 1830, might deplore autocratic rule and German disunity, but the local or 'particularist' interests were not artificial : they had long roots in the past, and were adaptable and resistant with a high facility for survival which had brought them through the perils of past centuries. Times were certainly changing, but many of the historic causes and results of disunity remained.

Germany had had no religious unity since the 16th century. She had no natural centre or capital city. Her frontiers were not defendable, and indeed in a strategical sense she had no frontiers. The mere fact of her position on the map had made her through the centuries the central battleground of European wars, the inevitable goal of expansive neighbours and military adventurers. Survival had often depended on the ability to be unobtrusive and deferential, and even to keep physically out of the way until the invading armies had passed on. Local units, the small principality or even the walled town had had the best chance of weathering these storms. This agelong disunity meant on the one hand the absence of national traditions or a common style or culture; even in language the small courts and governing classes had for long fav-

oured French. On the other hand it often meant a vigorous local life and local loyalties, not without their
attractions in peaceful times. Every small ruler after all
felt that he must provide his capital with an opera house.
But the dream of national greatness in unity had its
counter-attractions, particularly for those who were too
young to have identified themselves with the alternatives.

German liberalism as a political force also had many
and depressing weaknesses. It was essentially a product
of the universities. Its leaders were usually professors.
Ideas had been put into their heads by the French revolutionaries, English parliamentarians, and German think-
ers who taught respect for the right of the individual to
will his own imperatives of duty. Sometimes this took
concrete form in a demand for English parliamentary
institutions, and it was taken for granted that freedom of
speech, of the press, of conscience, of trial by jury were
the universal rights of free men. In the reactionary small
state the liberal and nationalist demands might go together, for the prince would be the opponent of both.
Some, too, were persuaded that a national German state
could exist only by popular consent and with representative institutions which would ensure the triumph of
liberalism. But in fact political liberalism on western
European lines never took deep roots. Numerically the
liberals were few in a land which was still largely one of
landlords and peasants, although they had supporters in
the small town middle classes and business circles and in
some circles of the country squirarchy. Romanticism, a
confusing and many-sided movement which appealed
widely to the emotions and generous sentiments of the
age, was the essential basis of the nationalist aspirations of
the student societies. Most of those who were moved by it
looked to a national state to revive the glories of a heroic
past rather than to establish free institutions.

Moreover in developing a theory of the state German
liberals, from a starting point in eighteenth century no-
tions of a natural order, favoured the principle that he
who governs least governs best. They denied the right of

the state to promote happiness in a positive way. Wilhelm von Humboldt said that states which seek to provide for the positive welfare of their citizens, 'resemble the physician who only retards the death of his patient in nourishing his disease'. State paternalism was harmful because it tended to destroy individual initiative and self-reliance. Some of the liberals still remembered their principles in the eighties, when they opposed Bismarck's social legislation. Humboldt and Fichte also found a solution for the liberal dilemma of the competing claims of individual rights and state duties. They preferred legal to political guarantees; providing the individual's basic rights were guaranteed by law in a *Rechtsstaat* (a state based on guaranteed legal rights) he should be prepared to render unto Caesar the initiative in policy. It is not surprising that even before the dose of realism that had to be swallowed by German liberals in 1848 there were some who had made their choice for a united Germany ruled by conservative Prussia rather than by a liberal constitution.

The Prussian officials, conscious of the obligations and unpopularity of the Prussian government, were also becoming aware of a new restlessness throughout the land. By the forties a generation was growing up in Germany which had been born too late to remember the horrors and upheavals of the Napoleonic wars. It was no longer so true as it had been in 1815 that the people, in the words of Metternich, preferred peace to liberty. The years of peace had strengthened men's nerves sufficiently to foster an increasing restiveness under their real or imagined grievances, and for the young there were battles—other people's battles—to be fought. In the Rhineland young Karl Marx, born 1818, the son of a Prussian official who wanted only a quiet life, entered the University of Bonn (which Bismarck would have liked to join) in 1835, also studied law, and also went on to finish his course at Berlin. He too distressed his parents by some duelling and drinking, and disappointed his mother by his failure to make progress in an orderly career. The two careers, soon to diverge towards the leadership of the two dominant ideologies of the modern world, are curiously alike in their initial circumstances and dissatisfactions. Both were soon to show a formidable irritation at the circumspection of their respective comrades in arms.

Bismarck's first taste of public life came almost accidently in 1847, when the new King of Prussia, Frederick William IV, summoned a joint meeting of the eight provincial diets of Prussia (*Landtage*) to meet in Berlin. This 'United Diet' was the nearest that the King was prepared to go towards the national representation which the Prussian people had been promised in 1815, and it would not have been called even in 1847 but for a royal order of 1820 saying that the King would not raise a public loan except with the consent of the estates of the realm. Bismarck missed the opening on 11 April for he was merely a reserve delegate, but a vacancy soon came and before the diet was closed at the end of June he had quickly and offensively established himself as the most die-hard Tory, the most mediaeval of Junkers, in Berlin. The majority were anything but advanced radicals or liberals, but they felt cheated of the constitutional advance which had been postponed for so long, and as a protest threw out the King's request for a loan to build the East Prussian railway.

In the tense and contentious atmosphere in which the diet displayed its well-meant but unproductive constitutionalism Bismarck's sarcasms and sharp tongue made an immediate impact. He denied that the Crown of Prussia needed any sanction other than the grace of God. He insisted on one occasion that Prussia had gone to war in 1813 to beat the French, not to gain a constitution. 'My performance produced a storm' he wrote complacently in his memoirs. Until it subsided he read a newspaper. Subsequently the King found it expedient to cut him at court functions. But when Bismarck, who had married a pious and homely woman, Johanna von Puttkamer, in July 1847, was on his honeymoon in Venice, the King recognized him and asked him to dinner. By this and

further invitations at Potsdam the King made it abundantly clear that his sturdy though somewhat embarrassing
young champion was in favour.

He was now 32. After the dissolution of the United
Diet and his father's death he had returned to his estates.
The meeting of the United Diet was an incident which
had done nothing to provide a life work. Nor did the
crowded and confused events of the revolutionary years,
from 1848 to 1850. He again played the part of the
intransigent extremist, making some more unpopular
speeches and dabbling unsuccessfully in 1848 in schemes
for counter-revolution; these forays and experiments
were more dramatic than practical, but they had their
bearing on his political outlook. For him as for many
other Germans the revolution provided a target and discredited all the apparent means of attaining it. In spite
of the fact that the movement culminated in the offer of
the imperial crown to the King of Prussia, Bismarck and
his conservative friends regarded it as unthinkable that
the unity of Germany even under Prussian leadership
should be the gift of a motley crowd of self-appointed
liberals, Reds, and radicals assembled at Frankfurt. But
the ideal of national unity was stronger than liberalism,
and the time would come when Bismarck himself would
be able to enlist the support of a chastened and reoriented
liberalism for his own German programme.

Risings in Paris in February 1848 soon had repercus-
sions in Germany and Austria, with a wave of more or less
spontaneous local insurrections and government changes.
In state after state liberal opposition leaders were called
on to form administrations, and many of the typical
liberal demands were granted. Although these liberal
leaders were of the middle class with a sprinkling of progressive noblemen they had peasant and working class
collaborators whose demands were soon tending to be
altogether too sweeping, republican, and generally embarrassing. There were peasant risings in many rural
districts during the first months of the year; they were
really due to the prolonged agricultural depression, but

they produced attacks on Jews and nobility as well as landlords, and frequent demands for a republic, following what was believed to be the American recipe for success. In the towns, and particularly in the Rhineland and Berlin, there were the authentic beginnings of modern communism among the small new class of industrial workers. Marx issued the *Communist Manifesto* and kindly set to work to 'abridge the hideous death agonies of capitalistic society' by stirring up as much trouble as possible with the help of his friend Friedrich Engels and the Communist League. There was also a social-radical movement in South Germany on the Jacobin model. In Berlin there was fighting on the barricades; news came of a successful revolution in Vienna, and after further demonstrations the King of Prussia promised concessions to the revolutionaries on 18 March 1848. A liberal ministry was formed under Ludolf Campenhausen. By the end of the month the more respectable middle class liberals had asserted themselves elsewhere and a large although self-appointed body met at Frankfurt am Main on 30 March and made arrangements for the election of a National Assembly. This met in St. Paul's Church in the city on 18 May amid great but decorous rejoicing. It was this orderly, liberal-minded, and patriotic body which later decided to offer the imperial crown to Frederick William.

The Frankfurt parliament failed, and for a reason which few German nationalists liked subsequently to face. It failed because there was not sufficient interest at this time in unity for its own sake : everyone concerned had a particularist or class or personal axe to grind first. The assembly set itself two tasks. One was to draw up a constitution for the whole of Germany. The other was to assert German nationality in its widest limits. The second of these aims was pursued partly because of the patriotic and somewhat intolerant nationalist ardour of many of the deputies; partly because it was hoped to provide a rallying cry for the whole country. The boundaries of 'Germany' were uncertain in every direction. There were German populations (as in France and Denmark) under non-German rule; there were non-German speaking minorities (as in Poland and Bohemia) under German rule. The Assembly, although not without debate and opposition, plumped whenever it could for the maximum advantage. It gave its blessing to Prussian military action against the Danes and the Poles, and to Austrian military action against the Czechs. The more extreme left groups, led by Robert Blum and Arnold Ruge, could only muster 31 votes against 342 for their support of Polish emancipation. But neither this assertive nationalism, nor the setting up of a central executive which could neither levy taxes nor control the armed forces of the member states, was sufficient to create an irresistible public movement in support of the first national government that Germany had possessed.

The members of the assembly were worthy men; all gentlemen, mostly of the middle and some of the upper middle class. They included 106 professors and teachers, 157 magistrates, 118 higher civil servants, with doctors, writers, some priests and pastors, and about a hundred business men and landowners. They had no popular roots, and looked askance at the dissatisfied peasantry, while the governments of the states looked askance at them. As soon as Frederick William recovered his nerve the days of the revolution were numbered. He was unbalanced, a romantic, never a liberal, although stirred by the nationalist enthusiasm. In the meantime the assembly itself had made the difficult decision to prefer a *Klein-deutsch* to a *Gross-deutsch* state; to prefer, that is to say, a Little Germany without Austria. There were those like the historians Dahlmann, Droysen, and Waitz who were hostile to Austria on principle as a disruptive force, and those who saw Protestantism and Prussia as the best foundations of the new state. But many were swayed by the practical consideration that the counter-revolution in Austria made Hapsburg co-operation with the Frankfurt parliament impossible. The constitution was based on universal, equal, and secret suffrage; a two chamber parliament, and government by an Emperor, whose orders were always to be countersigned by a minister. In the end, twenty-eight German states accepted the constitution, but Austria, Bavaria, and Hanover did not, and when the imperial title was offered to Frederick William in April 1849 he virtually rejected it by making his consent depend on that of his fellow German rulers. By the end of May 1849 all but a die-hard minority of the Frankfurt parliament had scattered to their homes.

This was the tragedy of German liberalism which Bismarck watched with curiosity, distaste, and a growing irritable sense that he could handle things better than his own leaders, given half a chance. He had established close links with an influential group of extreme conservatives in Berlin led by the brothers von Gerlach. General Leopold von Gerlach was the king's personal aide-de-camp and friend, and the group sought to use this intimacy to build up the King's resistance to the constitutional policy which the official ministry was trying to carry out. This group or *camarilla*, as it was called, had some successes, limited by the King's conviction of his own divinely-endowed insight. The influence of the Junkers was increased by the recently formed German Conservative party. Their daily paper, the *Kreuzzeitung*, for which Bismarck wrote numerous pungent, lively, but usually anonymous articles, propagated the party's views, and they had also found an able political theorist in Friedrich Julius Stahl, a professor in the University of Berlin, who gave some academic respectability to the anti-liberal position. Bismarck, although he was thinking always on practical lines, might be said to have shared Stahl's basic views. The effect of Stahl's theories was to confirm the Lutheran conception of the prince as properly holding power from God; he could not be dominated by a parliament, although neither Stahl nor Bismarck approved of unqualified absolutism. The estates should have the right of protest and consultation, but no more. Bismarck's ideal at this period was a wise and patriotic monarch, guided by his faithful Junkers; he distrusted the bourgeois liberal reformer and also the Prussian bureaucrat, the latter from personal experience. Nevertheless, he would support the aristocratic opposition to absolute monarchy in a clash between the two.

But for him as for so many Germans the 1848 revolution and its aftermath, while revealing the practical difficulties of any closer unification of the German states, made unity and the consequent problems of foreign policy the primary issue of Prussian politics for the future. He had no very clear idea as to how it should be brought about; but he already had strong views as to how it should not. While admitting in April 1849 in the debate on the Frankfurt constitution that everyone 'who speaks German wants German unity' he opposed the Frankfurt proposals because they sought to undermine and demolish the separate identity of Prussia, providing instead 'organized anarchy' in the shape of universal suffrage. But this did not rule out the possibility of a German state or federation in which Prussia would play the dominating part, after eliminating Austria. He thoroughly approved the King's contemptuous rejection of the proffered imperial title, but hoped that Prussia would 'give laws to Germany rather than receive them'. During the early summer of 1849 Prussian troops were busy in Prussia and other German states in suppressing popular risings in defence of the constitution, and he thought that this was Prussia's great opportunity; he continued to complain of its loss in after years.

We can say, therefore, that already by the summer of 1849 he had arrived at the conviction that a resolute ruler of Prussia, choosing the right moment and the right cause, could gain for Prussia the dominant power in Europe that was her due, and Germany's advantage; that a liberal constitution such as that of Frankfurt would stultify the power and experience that the Prussian monarchy and its ruling class must provide for Germany's good; and that the problem of Austria must be decided on empirical lines, in accordance with opportunity. In a speech in the Landtag on 6 September 1849 he asked bluntly what Frederick the Great would have done in the circumstances, and answered his own question. He would either have acted alone in dictating a constitution to Germany at the risk of war or he would have joined Austria in smashing liberal and nationalist revolution, the common enemy. Frederick William IV admitted he was no Frederick the Great.

But with the help of his friend, General von Radowitz, the King did make an attempt to devise a north German union of his own, consisting of Prussia and the four kingdoms of Bavaria, Württemberg, Hanover, and Saxony, together with the small German states. The union was to have a common parliament and a constitution, and would work closely with Austria, who would not, however, be a member. Bismarck seems to have distrusted this plan from the start, for it embodied liberal features and at the same time threatened war with Austria, now triumphant over her own rebels. Under Austrian pressure the four kingdoms seceded from the union, which however in its diminished form had a meeting of its parliament at Erfurt, and approved a draft constitution in April 1850. There followed an uneven contest between the Prussian government and Austria's forceful prime minister, Prince Schwarzenberg, who summoned a meeting of the Federal Diet of the old German Confederation, thus giving Saxony and Hanover an excuse for resigning from the Union. War seemed imminent in October. But the Tsar spoke in favour of the restoration of the German Confederation, and although the King of Prussia disliked giving way he deferred for once to the opinion of his cabinet, which believed that Prussia was not in a position to fight.

At the beginning of this final crisis Bismarck, at home in Schönhausen, was patriotically aggressive. Let war come, he said; 'every Prussian sabre will glisten high and joyfully in the sun'. But in November 1850 he was recalled both to his regiment and to the next session of the Landtag, and after a talk with General Stockhausen, the Minister of War, he changed his mind and supported the terms which Austria demanded of Prussia at Olmütz on 28 November 1850, and which were completed by an

Austro–Prussian military alliance in 1851. In a speech of 3 December he called for 'Prussia's abstinence before all things from every shameful union with democracy', and looked forward to the joint execution with equal authority by Austria and Prussia, the two protecting powers of Germany, of whatever they might think reasonable.

This was sheer expediency, an attempt to help out the government, which considered itself (perhaps wrongly) not to be in a position to fight. It is an early example of his ability to bridle his natural pugnacity in the state interest. He liked to think of himself as a fighter, but calculation dominated his actions throughout his career, although he was often emotionally irked—with a trail of smashed vases, wrenched doorknobs, tears, and resignation threats to mark the crises—by the need to control passion by reason. He was a man of instinctive violence saved by his intelligence. This taught him to give it safe outlets. When he found a career, care for his own advancement added to his circumspection, although he remained, in the eyes of his contemporaries, a violent man.

And at last he received a reward for his exertions and loyalty. In April 1851, just after his 36th birthday, he was appointed Prussian envoy to the revived German Bund at Frankfurt. He knew little of the routine of diplomatic business. But he was otherwise familiar enough with the demands of public life; by now a practised and formidable speaker, he was socially at ease and even a figure of some influence in Court circles, very much in the inner ring of royal and ultra-conservative politics, and intimately involved in their intrigues and aspirations. His courageous, not to say aggressive, personality would be an asset in view of Prussia's unpopularity and isolation in the Confederation. How far this influenced the King's choice, which was made on the advice of Leopold von Gerlach, is not clear. Bismarck and the *camarilla* regarded it as a pledge that the government had finally renounced the revolution, and also that it was ready to work with Austria in what was ostensibly a return to pre-revolutionary politics. So he threw himself with zest into the curious political struggle at Frankfurt, in which the Prussian envoy's personal accomplishments had to compensate in some degree for the anomalous position of his country. He was to remain there for eight years, and if at the end of it Prussia's position in German politics was not very different from what it had been at the beginning his embassy was still important for what it taught him, if not for what it achieved.

The single dominating impulse throughout his career was the exercise of power. His mind responded to the challenge of problems in every sphere of public life, and although his political friendships and youthful associations had given him strong links with conservative Prussia he was to show himself prepared in the last resort to subordinate any interest to the overriding needs of the state, as he conceived them. It would be over-simplifying the position to see him as a mere careerist. He was a passionate and dogmatic man in many ways, much given to ruminations about his duty and his conscience, and we must assume the existence of basic loyalties which remained unshakable by the needs of opportunism. But certain of these—Prussia, the dynasty, the Lutheran church —were so much bound up with his own position after 1862 that the question of their being thrown overboard could never arise. Apart from these fundamentals he was consciously a machiavellian statesman, coolly analysing alternative courses, suiting his action to the needs of policy, putting success before consistency.

But he was also a man of ranging curiosity and tremendous zest for activity, and this gave him, on the one hand, great flexibility and charm of manner when he chose to exercise it in conquering the goodwill of people right outside his own circle, and, on the other, the ability to explore and grasp the diverse possibilities of men and movements. The more we study his career the more interesting becomes his early life, with its restless urge to see things, read everything, learn languages, and enjoy an existence far removed from that of the struggling Junker farmer. The divergent streams of Prussian life could not be easily reconciled, and he was contemptuous of the futile efforts of the professors at Frankfurt. But he was perfectly willing to utilize the slogans of liberalism, quotations from Goethe, the solvent of the national appeal, to reinforce the forward policy of the Prussian state, just as he was prepared to advocate and later to practise a complete objectivity in the cultivation and dropping of foreign allies. And this meant in turn that in spite of the decisive impetus that he could give to public developments by his personal practical ability he was ultimately their servant; by adapting himself to existing conditions he was himself governed by them. Germany, we might say, got the Bismarck she deserved.

During the fifties he gained the indispensable self-confidence which enabled him to think with growing impatience of his ultimate mastery of power, and along with this a great many tough and not very practicable plans were turning over in his mind and being tried out on his rather unsympathetic superiors. The fifties were a period of quiescence and anti-climax after the revolutionary excitements, and this dynamism was embarrassing.

It was also the decade of Germany's first real rendezvous with her economic destiny in the shape of the industrial revolution, with the doubling or trebling of coal and iron production, the rapid growth of railways, factories, slums, and joint stock companies, the consequent creation of an industrial proletariat, and a substantial strengthening of the bourgeoisie in wealth and numbers. Population increased from 36,000,000 to 38,000,000 in spite of widespread emigration after the economic distress and political disappointments of the forties. Agriculture shared for a time in the advance, and while exports of grain increased the more enterprising landowners, including the Bismarcks, promoted such rural industries as sugar refineries and saw mills on their estates. But although the future of German socialism was assured by the creation of a vast urban working class, the lack of organization and the habit of obedience in a well-drilled military state prevented any immediate proletarian impact on politics. Liberal elements in the expanding middle class on the other hand had recently had a surfeit of politics, and were not disposed to renew their revolutionary activity. They were largely disillusioned, and if they had the choice might well prefer national unity to political liberty. The professors went back to their universities and played little further part as political leaders.

In the smaller states the rulers had reasserted their authority, usually in its old repressive forms, but their assurance was shaken, and the Confederation no great comfort. The Austrians behind their bravado were not very sure of themselves. In Prussia the prime minister (1850–59) was Otto von Manteuffel, who had negotiated the Olmütz agreement, a patient reactionary under whose direction the liberal achievements of the revolutionary era were whittled away. Frederick William did not abolish the constitution which he had granted; but it was reissued with drastic revisions on 30 January 1850. In place of universal suffrage an indirect system of election to the diet by three classes was devised, with the votes weighed heavily in favour of the landed and business classes. This as it happened was a blunder; the idea was to rely on the propertied classes, with the greatest stake in stability, but among these were some of the main supporters of liberalism. The Progressive party in Prussia, the bulwark of liberalism, was founded in 1861 by East Prussian landowners who were devotees of free trade and constitutional government.

It was essentially the Junkers who benefited most. In due course they regained their privileged position in local government, and the elected members of the Upper House were so reduced that after 1854 it was mainly composed of landed nobility. Independent and liberal-minded politicians were harried by the police, prosecuted with perjured evidence, sometimes driven from their jobs, and handicapped by restrictions on the freedom of the press. After 1855 officials predominated in the membership of the Lower House, and although many of these were liberally inclined they could be subjected to pressure through their employment. This course of things provided a good advertisement for the liberals and moderate conservatives. A small but distinguished group of the latter produced a weekly paper, *Das preussische Wochenblatt*, in opposition to the *Kreuzzeitung*, and the King's brother, Prince William of Prussia, who disliked the Olmütz settlement and many features of the reaction, was known to regard the *Wochenblatt* group with some favour. But during the greater part of the fifties the government wanted no reforms and no adventures, and the Berlin police chief, Hinckeldey, was a dominant and typical and much hated figure until someone killed him in a duel.

So although Bismarck speedily established his standing as a determined and at times highly exasperating opponent of the Austrian representative at Frankfurt he could not interest the government in many of his ideas for Prussia's aggrandisement. These soon begin to appear in his voluminous correspondence, particularly with Manteuffel and von Gerlach, together with many suggestions as to the proper utilization of diplomatic opportunities. If he had had any genuine belief in the possibility of Prussian co-operation with Austria he lost it within a week of taking up his duties, and his first moves were directed towards the establishment of Prussia's full equality of status with Austria in the Confederation. It seemed clear that the Austrian government, which had usually been prepared to consult the Prussians before putting proposals to the Diet in Metternich's day, was now more arrogant and disinclined to treat Prussia differently from the other members. Bismarck found it convenient to start with such trivialities as his right to smoke cigars at meetings of the diet, where for some reason only the Austrian delegate as president had hitherto done so. He also declined to be kept waiting when he called on the president. He made himself awkward by obstructing Austrian proposals in the Diet and set to work to build up support for Prussia among the smaller states. Whether this did Prussia any particular good is rather doubtful, for the governments of the smaller states were as determined to resist Prussian as they were Austrian encroachments. But he did manage to upset the Austrian delegate, Count Thun, and his successor, Count Prokesch-Osten. A diplomatic mission to Vienna in 1852 enabled him to study the makeshift Hapsburg governmental methods at first hand.

Bismarck's more positive plans were based on force and, rather less emphatically, on the satisfaction of the material interests of those smaller German states within Prussia's field of interest which he believed could be tied to Prussia by treaties in the style of the Zollverein. His most strongly held view was that in order to subdue Austria and dominate the German states Prussia must seek the support of France. Before the end of 1852 he had begun to advise against any quarrel with Napoleon III, and as the Crimean war (1853–6) revolutionized European state relations he pressed his government more and more insistently to take advantage of Austria's isolation.

The Prussian government was not prepared to force a quarrel on Austria, and although the Austrian pretensions were resented at times the general tendency of Prussian policy was to come to Austria's support when she was in trouble. During the Crimean war, Frederick William IV was on the whole loyal to the Austrian alliance, although anxious not to get into trouble either with Russia or with the western powers who were fighting her. He renewed the Prussian military alliance with Austria in April 1854, but was evidently pleased when the lesser states in the German Confederation refused to accept Austria's plans for mobilizing the army of the Confederation against Russia in 1855. Thus Prussia might be said to have followed a somewhat ignominious policy of non-involvement during the struggle, but the western powers had nothing to complain of in her conduct, and Russia was grateful for her neutrality. Bismarck had been alarmed lest she be dragged into war, but otherwise his chief concern was that she should not estrange either Russia or France,

whose post-war friendship he foresaw very astutely. The
King was incapacitated by a stroke in October 1857, and
his brother Prince William acted as his deputy and then
as Regent until the King's death and his own accession
to the throne in 1861. It was, accordingly, to Prince William that Bismarck addressed his arguments, but when
they were finally rejected by the prince in 1858 he knew
that his career was probably at an end.

We can sum up his political ideas at this point by saying that he was convinced of two things : the first was that
Austria must somehow be forced to agree to the expansion
of Prussian influence in Germany; the second was that
Prussia must find support outside Germany in order to
coerce Austria. The second of these aims shows that he
was not counting at this stage on the ability of the Prussian army to defeat Austria singlehanded. He was thinking far more of the benefit that Prussia could derive from
a Franco–Russian quarrel with Austria, although only if
she had the foresight to join the winners before their
victory.

As the idea of foreign support was repugnant to the
Regent, Bismarck did not stress it when he made his
crowning effort to prescribe the foreign policy of the
government in March 1858. He brought forward instead
the bold idea, very different from his early views, of an
appeal to German nationalist sentiment over the heads
of any conservatively-minded princes as a means of rallying support to Prussian foreign policy. However, the
Regent had other plans. He dismissed the reactionary
bureaucrat Manteuffel and chose a new cabinet from the
Wochenblatt group and the liberal opposition in the
Prussian chamber. They were to introduce a 'new era' in
policy, which meant in practice some mild reforms and a
better moral tone in public life, without, however, any
encroachment on the royal authority or the constitution.
The new prime minister was Prince Charles Anthony of
Hohenzollern-Sigmaringen. Neither Baron Alexander von
Schleinitz, the new foreign minister, nor the Regent himself was attracted by Bismarck's adventurous proposals;

they preferred peace and co-operation with Austria and Great Britain.

So the period of Bismarck's diplomatic apprenticeship ends with his removal from Frankfurt; he was hardly the best agent for the new attempt at Austro–Prussian *rapprochement*. Robert von Keudell, one of his close associates, thought that he had grown in stature at Frankfurt, and was no longer a party politician. 'His independent surveys of the situation at home and abroad, his bold designs, his manly character, brought stimulus and refreshment of spirit.' But he was sent as ambassador to St. Petersburg in March 1859; put in cold storage on the Neva in his own sardonic words. He had established himself as the masterful extremist of Prussian politics, the troubleshooter who could only await the call for action.

But at first the likelihood of any call seemed doubtful. When Austria fought France and Sardinia in the summer of 1859 the Prussian government did everything wrong according to Bismarck's ideas. The Regent was loyal to Austria after his fashion, but could get no promise of concessions in return for his support, and finally mobilized the army for no very clear reason just when the fighting was coming to an end. Prussia played no more part in the peace settlement (the treaty of Villafranca) in 1859 than she had done in that of 1856. Hesitant and mediocre diplomacy, in Bismarck's eyes, and he saw little hope that the government would take advantage of the nationalist enthusiasm which was beginning to revive, stimulated by the unification of north Italy. The Italian successes encouraged a group of North German liberals to form the *Deutscher Nationalverein* (German National Union) in September 1859, after some preliminary conferences. Although generally liberal in politics its members wanted to strengthen the Confederation, they looked to Prussia for leadership, and they were in the main *kleindeutsch*, although with hopes of some amicable arrangement with Austria. The president was Rudolf von Bennigsen, the leader of the liberal opposition in Hanover; it included from the start many of the great names of German democratic politics in the coming years, such as Schulze-Delitzsch, Viktor von Unruh, Johannes Miquel, and others. It drew its membership from the usual professional, business, and official circles; at the height of its influence in 1862 it numbered only 25,000; but as the first German party on national lines it had a significant although troubled place in Bismarck's later plans.

He was disappointed, even a little soured, by his change of post. His health for the first time failed him, and if his astonishing self-confidence remained, something of the spontaneous offensiveness and arrogant outpouring of ideas had been abandoned. 'I feel like an old-age pensioner,' he wrote to his sister, 'who has finished with the work of this world.' His age was approximately that of President John F. Kennedy at his Inauguration, or of Napoleon at Waterloo. Early in 1861 a junior attaché, Friedrich von Holstein, who as a child had known Bismarck as a young and jovial visitor to his father's home, found him unsmiling and withdrawn. His picture of Bismarck at St. Petersburg is of a dissatisfied man, partly a hypochondriac, missing the constant strife of Frankfurt, shunning the society of his diplomatic colleagues (most of whom bored him) but not omitting to cultivate the goodwill of the Tsar, Alexander II, and the Russian Chancellor, Prince Gorchakov. He took exercise, walking or riding, every day, but did not really lead a healthy life, for he relied mainly on one enormous late meal, at which he ate and drank far too heavily. The fact that he could continue this unbalanced diet for another twenty years was a tribute to his constitution, but his frequent 'black moods' were often physical in origin. Holstein remarks that he had 'scarcely even known anyone so joyless as Bismarck'.

However, the young attaché was scarcely in a position at this stage of his career to penetrate the deeper reaches of Bismarck's personality and ambitions. In Prussia the 'new era' pleased no one very much, and Bismarck soon recovered his hopes of advancement. He was considered for the post of foreign minister in the spring of 1860, when he happened to be convalescing in Berlin after a severe bout of rheumatic fever. The Regent could not bring himself to make the appointment, but knew that he might have to call on his most forceful servant before long. Bismarck was again considered in 1861, and again sent back to Petersburg because William (who had been King of Prussia since January) hesitated to accept the robust consequences, but all the time his difficulties with the parliamentary opposition were mounting. Bismarck for his part had not deviated from his basic aim of Prussian mastery of Germany in defiance of Austria, but with the cooling of the Franco–Russian friendship in the late fifties and with Prince William's hostility to France in mind he had to choose his ground carefully. He came out strongly in July 1861, in the 'Baden-Baden memorial', in favour of German nationalism as the moral basis of Prussian expansion. His more specific proposal was for a '*Zollverein* parliament', which would give the states linked together in the *Zollverein* a representative assembly and military organization; they might not like it, and Austria certainly would not, but he believed that skilful—in other words, Bismarckian—leadership would bring it about.

The King again shied away from such virile plans, but while he was unwilling to quarrel with Austria (in spite of his growing annoyance with her) he was moving rapidly to a deadlock with the Prussian liberals which at last brought his 'red reactionary' to office.

Chapter Two

The First Successes

BISMARCK'S appointment as minister-president and foreign minister of Prussia on 24 September 1862 was an act of bravado by a defeated man. King William had stubbornly refused to compromise on plans for the reorganization of the Prussian army. By 19 September he seemed to be faced with the choice between abdication, a military dictatorship, and surrender to the demands of the majority in the chamber of deputies. He was supported by General Edwin von Manteuffel (cousin of Otto von Manteuffel), the real implacable extremist among the soldiers, head of the personnel division of the war ministry and chief of the military cabinet. This group owed its influence to the fact that the King, as commander of the armed forces, took the view that his responsibilities in this field could not be delegated even to the minister of war. It was ready for a military dictatorship. General Albrecht von Roon, minister of war since 1859, did have to speak for the government on military matters in parliament, and he had, like Manteuffel, direct access to the King; the other ministers could do so only through the minister-president. Roon and Manteuffel were agreed on the present issues, but Roon was bound to distrust the continued efforts of the military cabinet to form a state within the state, and to be free even of the indirect control of parliament through the minister of war.

So the King, encouraged by his military die-hards, defied the deputies. His son, the Crown Prince Frederick William, urged surrender, for although he wanted the military reforms he did not think the final point at issue, the difference between two and three years' service, worth an abdication or a military dictatorship (which the army chiefs would have been happy to supply). The deputies were not men of violence, and did not oblige the generals by mounting any revolutionary barricades. But Prussia had a constitution, and parliament could refuse the budget. It was in these circumstances that the advocacy of von Roon, Bismarck's sole supporter, succeeded. Bismarck was interviewed; and he assured the King, striking the right note, that he would do his duty as a feudal vassal unconditionally faithful to his lord. Touched and aroused by this sturdy declaration of loyalty, the King decided to fight on, and quite forgot to tie Bismarck down to any particular programme.

The resolution with which Bismarck held his new post and used it to carry out an adventurous foreign policy with resounding success places him among the supreme masters of modern politics, and there is no doubt as to the verdict of history in this respect. Nor can there be much doubt that while he made at first some false moves and continued to make unnecessary enemies his peculiar gifts and temperament were well suited to the conditions of Prussian politics in the sixties. He was to reveal extraordinary tactical skill in political and diplomatic manoeuvre, an almost insolent self-assurance among a great many dithery and irresolute colleagues, and the ability to discern latent advantages in the most awkward situations both at home and abroad. But can we say that in turning these circumstances to the best advantage he was forcing on Prussia and Germany a choice in favour of militant nationalism and perhaps other unpleasant things which otherwise they would never have accepted? This is to attribute too great a mastery of events even to Bismarck. It is true that he was a man of domineering and autocratic temperament, 'a rough man even in politics' as one of his contemporaries put it, and that much of what he did took a peculiar form in response to his unique character and personality. He boasted on one occasion that he learnt his diplomacy in the horse-fairs of Pomerania. But as we follow the story of his struggles we soon

have to abandon the notion of a mere forceful reactionary, for not only did he show remarkable ability in adapting himself to the requirements of public business but he
was singularly free from bondage or even loyalty to any
man or idea or institution that stood in his way.

With no appreciable support from any political group
or party, Bismarck to begin with needed the backing of
the King exactly as the King needed him, and until William had accustomed himself to the idea that this wild
man could in fact govern the state successfully there was
every likelihood that a settlement of the differences with
the chamber would lead to his dismissal. On the other
hand, Bismarck could see that the attitude of blank defiance and open deadlock which existed at the moment
of his appointment must somehow be relaxed. He fully
shared the objections of the King and the Conservatives
to the 'constitutional state' but with his mind always
turning to the needs of external policy he regarded a
paralysing domestic conflict as undesirable and his ultimate aim was a loyal but subservient chamber which
would leave the King (and therefore his ministers) free to
exercise the residual authority which he still possessed.
Ignoring therefore the short-sighted view that it was to
his advantage to prolong the constitutional crisis he
sought during the first weeks of office, and with the collaboration of Roon, a complicated compromise settlement
ingeniously and energetically supported by persuasive
talk adapted to the outlook of all the parties concerned.

Although this plan failed it had the incidental effect
of strengthening his hold on the King. On 23 September
the chamber had finally defied the King by striking out
of the budget the amount needed for the military reorganization. As a gesture of conciliation Bismarck first
withdrew the budget proposals for the following year,
1863, and sought in private talks with the liberal leaders
to persuade them that he was himself a reasonable man
of liberal outlook, that he stood between the country and
complete reaction, and that a prolongation of the conflict
between crown and parliament could only weaken the

country abroad. He hinted that he could bring the King round to the acceptance of the two-year term if the liberal leaders were patient and co-operative. To Karl Twetsen, a moderate liberal who disliked the prospect of a constitutional struggle, he spoke of the King as a horse that shied but could be trained. While he dangled these prospects of an honourable *dénouement* before the unwarlike liberals he was assuring the magnates of the upper chamber that he would follow a policy of stern reaction if necessary, and for the King himself there were further stout affirmations of his unflinching resolution.

Against the background of his talks to the liberal leaders (of which the King was unaware) Bismarck's first speech to the Chamber on 30 September, delivered in his unusual rapid, uneven, high pitched tones, must have been something of a puzzle. He spoke of his desire for a settlement, but allowed his main preoccupation to show itself in talking about Prussia's tasks and the future. Prussia carried a weight of arms too great for her frail body. Now she would use it to the full. Her boundaries were not favourable to a healthy state life. The great questions of the time were not decided by speeches and majority decisions, but by 'iron and blood'. To Bismarck this famous phrase—which became transposed in usage —was not a declaration of war on anyone, but a plain statement of fact. Some of his hearers—including Roon and the King—were shocked by his belligerence, and some by his indiscretion. The King's nerves were so strained that he could be heard in the street in Baden-Baden yelling at his son-in-law who had incautiously discussed the events of 1849. During a railway journey on 4 October Bismarck found the King morosely contemplating the death of Louis XVI. But he rallied his master with inspiring words, and called on him to think instead of the nobler fate of Charles I. 'You must oppose tyranny, even if you incur bodily harm!' The appeal was wonderfully successful; the Hohenzoller remembered his duty, assumed a joyful and warlike bearing, and what is

more, converted Bismarck's appointment, hitherto temporary, into a definite nomination.

The King's confirmation of his position was the decisive fact for Bismarck; as his hopes of squaring the constitutional circle by a quick clever compromise faded, he
felt strong enough to take a more defiant line towards
the opposition. On the other hand the King's strengthened resolution made him even less ready to accept any
compromise on the military question that suggested surrender to his simple mind. On 10 October Roon put
forward an ingenious plan under which conscripts could
purchase release after two years, but would otherwise
serve a third year, and the army would be of a fixed size
(one per cent of the population), with an agreed sum for
each soldier. This would rule out the annual voting of
military expenditure, and was expected to attract the
bourgeoisie, who could buy their release from the compulsory third year. Bismarck had left Roon to argue the
matter out with the King, but had hoped that the plan
would prove sufficiently attractive at least to divide the
liberals in parliament. However, the King, advised by
the military cabinet, objected to every substantial concession.

The upper house, on Bismarck's prompting, threw out
the budget which the lower house had amended on 23
September, and voted it in its original form; he then
announced that in view of the deadlock for which the
constitution made no provision the King would have to
dispose of the revenues of the state until an agreement
had been reached. In other words, he would govern without consent of parliament. The constitutional position
was much nearer to that of the English King in Parliament in the sixteen-thirties, than of contemporary politics
in the eighteen-sixties; English liberals were thus inclined
to horrified but somewhat misjudged denunciations of
his 'devilish sophistries' and to prophesies of his inevitable
disaster. It is true that his theory of a gap in the constitution (the so-called *Lückentheorie*) convinced no one, least
of all himself; but although the political immorality of

Bismarck's actions was gravely denounced by the eminent lawyer, Professor Gneist, and others, nothing much else could be done. Roon's emasculated military proposals were, however, rejected in the new year. After this Bismarck ruled in defiance of the lower house until 1866.

Success—and indeed survival—now depended entirely on his achievements in foreign policy. His mind had been running for so many years on the rivalry with Austria and the ways and means of Prussian domination of north Germany that these would have been his main concern even if domestic affairs had been no problem. But foreign policy had now to serve a double purpose. For the next twelve months he was hunting around for a suitable issue, and making little progress and some mistakes, while his liberal opponents maintained their opposition and their popularity. In his memoirs thirty years later he could not resist the temptation to present his career as a record of triumphant moves towards a series of well-defined objectives. Doubtless the chances and ambiguities of the way ahead are easily forgotten in retrospect by any old man looking back on a crowded life, and Bismarck liked a good tale, told by himself preferably, at other people's expense. But the road ahead did not reveal itself with any clarity at the beginning. In the process of feeling his way forward he followed more than one path; he was already skilled in the art of keeping alternative negotiations in progress in order to maintain his freedom of choice, and he was not at all disturbed by accusations of duplicity. He was sure that the Prussian liberals would rally to the monarchy in sufficient numbers after a great national triumph. The 'blood and iron' speech had been merely a rather too obvious attempt, based on this conviction, to divert their attention from the domestic issues. They too were content to await a double success, for on their side they believed that a national triumph would be a popular liberal triumph and would destroy the reactionary Junker, who would never be able to command the support of the masses. Bismarck believed differently, and was even prepared to turn to a popular appeal in the

form of universal suffrage in the belief that the liberals
had no sure hold on mass opinion. He looked for support
more hopefully, however, to German liberals outside
Prussia.

There was already talk of war with Austria within
three months of Bismarck's attainment of office. But the
hope of using French and possibly Russian goodwill to
isolate Austria quickly faded. He was himself forced onto
the defensive, and for the next twelve months could do
little in the German question beyond fending off Austria's
attempts to strengthen her influence. This she was at-
tempting to do in two related spheres.

In the commercial field she had been promised in 1853
that Prussia would negotiate with her over the possibility
of her joining the *Zollverein* before the existing treaties
expired in 1865, and she boldly put forward plans (in
1862) for a great central European customs union stretch-
ing from the North Sea to the Adriatic. Under this
common-market system Austrian industry would be
bound to suffer when faced with the competition of that
of Prussia, Saxony, and Bavaria, but the Habsburg government was prepared for the economic loss in return for
the political gain. Consequently it was justifiably annoyed
when in March 1862 Prussia concluded a new commercial
treaty with France, which if ratified by the other *Zollverein* states would defeat the Austrian plans. This was
the position when Bismarck came into office. With his
hopes of using the *Zollverein* as the basis for a political
union he had no intention of agreeing to the Austrian
proposals; it was difficult nevertheless to deny that Prussia
had gone back on her promise of 1853. Austria was also
able to draw encouragement from the fact that some of
Prussia's *Zollverein* partners were unenthusiastic about
the treaty; they confirmed it however in October (Bismarck's first success in foreign policy). Austria's counter
pressure dragged on until the autumn of 1864. Austria
also hoped to improve her position in the Confederation.

The many proposals that were being discussed at this

time for the reform of the Confederation, all with the purpose of satisfying in some degree the nationalist aspirations of the German people, show that there certainly were alternatives to the blood and iron solution. Something could probably have been done by agreement to provide a strengthened direction of central affairs, and Prussia's natural importance as the dominant power, in both economic and military matters, among the northern states would have given her a decisive voice in the really important issues. But an agreed solution would only be possible with the inclusion of Austria, and Bismarck and all his colleagues were convinced that she would never cede the position of dominant partner.

Bismarck had made his own proposals in the Baden-Baden memorial in the summer of 1861, and in September 1861 King William and his foreign minister Count Bernstorff (who had recently succeeded Schleinitz), had agreed with Franz von Roggenbach, the foreign minister of Baden, to a plan for reform which was to set up a federal union of the north German states with a national parliament within the older Confederation. The executive would be Prussian. The Habsburg dominions would be guaranteed. King William had, however, a strong sense of duty to the other German princes and of loyalty to the Emperor and had been pressing since 1859 for a reform of the military organization of the Confederation; he wanted to command the confederate army or at least to control it in northern Germany, and if this had been promptly conceded he might well have accepted some *grossdeutsch* solution. But the Austrians disliked any strengthening of Prussian influence and felt that they might be able to take advantage of the Prussian internal crisis to push through a plan for setting up a central committee representing all the governments of the Confederation. This was proposed in September 1861, and in December 1861 Prussia showed its dislike of this solution by putting forward its own plan for a smaller northern confederation within the larger one. But Bernstorff did not feel strong enough to insist on this arrangement, which was so reminiscent of Radowitz's constitution of 1850, and Austria continued to press her own views; there was much speculation as to whether Prussia would again have to submit to an humiliating surrender, another Olmütz in fact.

As soon as he came into office in October 1862, Bismarck made it clear that he too was opposed to the Austrian proposals; and in doing so he was merely continuing Bernstorff's policy, although in a more truculent spirit. All the Prussian ministers were agreed that Prussia would always be at a disadvantage under an arrangement whereby she could be isolated by Austria relying on the votes of the smaller states. He visited Napoleon III in October to say farewell on quitting the Paris embassy, and having satisfied himself (rather too hastily) that France would not interfere in an Austro–Prussian war, at once told the Austrian ambassador in Paris that he intended to establish Prussian leadership in northern Germany and to use any available means to gain his ends should Austria oppose him. He repeated this warning to the Austrian ambassador in Berlin in December, only to find the Austrian foreign minister, Count Rechberg, frostily unresponsive. This challenge was accompanied by hints that he would if necessary rely on French help, but also by assurances that he would prefer a solid alliance in which Prussia on her part would guarantee Austria's position in Italy and the Balkans. Thus his more menacing attitude was adroitly mixed with offers and enticements; he was leaving the door ajar for some agreement with Austria if the need arose. France indeed made it clear in December that she had no intention of giving Prussia a free hand in Germany.

Just before this Bismarck had marched troops into Kassel in support of the Hessian parliament, which the Elector was defying as usual, very much as Bismarck himself was doing in Berlin. But the Elector promptly gave way, and Bismarck was unable to make much use of his intervention as a means of frightening the smaller states. However, they were sufficiently influenced by his admonitions and warnings, which included the threat that Prussia would withdraw from the Diet in protest if need be. The Austrian proposals were accordingly rejected by nine votes to seven in January 1863.

No one can possibly argue from all this that Austria was not doing everything in her power to secure the leadership of Germany in a reformed Confederation, and there is no appreciable difference between Bismarck and Bernstorff apart from his fiercely optimistic will to achieve the Prussian ends by force or manoeuvre. If the Austrians were persistent their tactics were mediocre, and they had yet to understand that Bismarck's impetuosity could win him friends as well as enemies. The shifting pattern of European politics had not yet given him a situation which he could successfully exploit, but he was trying everything.

As it happened his first major opportunity in foreign affairs presented itself on the day that the Austrian proposal was rejected by the Diet. But on this occasion he misjudged his chances, and perhaps can be said to have come out of the crisis rather better than he deserved. It was known on 22 January 1863 that a large scale insurrection had broken out in Russian Poland over the question of conscription. Bismarck immediately moved four army corps into Prussian Poland, which was not affected by the rising, and General von Alvensleben was sent to St. Petersburg to discuss joint measures with the Russians. All this was later interpreted as a farsighted and well-timed move on his part to win Russia's friendship. But he seems to have been influenced mainly by alarm at the effect of any Polish successes on Prussia's own Polish population, whom she could never afford to liberate. He was particularly concerned at the report of plans, which Gorchakov himself was believed to favour, for the setting up of an independent or autonomous Polish state. This Prussia's own Polish subjects would wish to join, and it would be certain to seek a French alliance. So agitated was he at this prospect that he determined to occupy the Russian area himself if Russia withdrew, and he was even

rash enough to take soundings in London, Paris, and
Vienna to this effect.

The Russian government were not flattered by Bismarck's suggestion that it needed help, and it was only
because the Tsar was unwilling to hurt the feelings of the
King of Prussia that the Alvensleben convention, providing for co-operation in the pursuit of rebels across the
joint frontier, was signed on 8 February 1863. It drew
on Prussia the immediate protests of London, Paris, and
Vienna, and Napoleon III, embarrassed by his desire to
retain the friendship of Russia while satisfying popular
sympathy in France for the Poles, was only too glad to
turn his diplomatic artillery against Berlin. Alarmed at
this hostility, and with a possibility before him of war
with Britain and France, Bismarck apparently offered his
resignation on 23 February 1863, and after Gorchakov
had assured him that Russia was quite willing to drop
the convention, told the British ambassador that it was
unlikely to come into force.

The fact is that Russo-Prussian friendship continued
in spite of Bismarck's intervention, rather than because
of it. The Tsar privately remarked 'our dear Bismarck is
a terrible blunderer'. But he was a friend, and although
his clumsiness was deplored it did not seem at all desirable
to the Russians that he should go, and be replaced by
some very much less co-operative prime minister. Moreover, although Gorchakov was mainly concerned to limit
Bismarck's humiliation (he was to become less sympathetic
in later years) he could not deny that there were advantages for Russia in having Prussia as a friendly buffer
between herself and the western powers, in the somewhat
unlikely event of their active intervention.

Lord Palmerston, the British prime minister, had in
fact turned down flatly Napoleon's proposal for such
action against Prussia, but from the beginning of March,
Great Britain, with the somewhat sulky support of France,
was concentrating her protests on the conduct of Russia,
which was after all the government mainly involved.
There was talk of their fighting Russia in the spring.

Austria dithered, and, as in the Crimean war, annoyed
the Russians without really joining the western powers.
Bismarck, now noticeably more cautious, was content to
say that he would have to await events, but he also said
that he would personally advise the King to support
Russia in the event of war. By the summer it had become
clear that Russia would have her way; the Poles were
gradually suppressed, the western protests ineffectually
died away, and Austria had pleased no one in particular.
Bismarck remained, in Russian eyes, a good friend.

But there was still no improvement in his prospects.
There was no real weakening of the opposition at home,
and Austria continued to push her case for the reform of
the Confederation, confident that Prussia's difficulties
over Poland had weakened her opposition. The plan that
now emerged was a development of that put forward in
1862. It had been very carefully worked out by the Emperor's advisers, and its main feature was a small direc-
torate with executive powers, consisting of six members,
who were to include the Emperor and the Kings of
Prussia and Saxony. There was to be an assembly of delegates elected by the chambers of the individual states. A
great meeting of German princes at Frankfurt, presided
over by the Emperor, was to ratify the plan.

Could the King of Prussia possibly resist the invitation,
which the Emperor flatteringly presented in person? Bismarck was determined that he should do so, and he stuck
at the King's side during August in a series of meetings
in Gastein, Baden-Baden, and Coburg until the famous
culminating interview at which the King tearfully gave
way, and Bismarck went home and smashed a vase and
cried with relief at his triumph. The Austrian plan was
doomed by William's abstention; there was again talk of
war, and the Russians were alarmed to find that Bismarck
appeared to favour it as a means of escape from his internal difficulties. But their first impulse, which was to maintain neutrality in the Austro–Prussian differences, was
followed once again by the reflection that there was no
satisfactory alternative to Bismarck, and in September the

Tsar, while making it clear that Russia could not support Prussia in war, promised to do all he could to restrain Vienna. So the Confederation remained unchanged, Prussia and Austria glowered at each other in resentful frustration, and the German liberals continued their futile dreams of a national unity which neither would dominate. But now at last the European situation began to move in Bismarck's favour, although not in the first instance as a result of any action on his part.

The Schleswig–Holstein–Lauenburg problem was one of those border issues, involving mixed populations, conflicting legal claims, and the ambiguities of political geography, which so often gave predatory German governments a case for war from Frederick the Great's invasion of Silesia in 1741 to Hitler's invasion of Poland in 1939. Being almost completely devoid of recognizable geographical boundaries the German people had no frontiers other than those of culture, i.e. language; to many it seemed self-evident that ultimately the nation-state should extend as far as the German tongue, 'so weit die deutsche Zunge klingt', in the words of Arndt's battle-hymn of 1813. Being in the midst of a singularly frustrating political battle in 1863 as to which combination of their members could safely be admitted to a reformed Confederation, the lesser German states were mainly concerned at the moment with the problem of unity, rather than of expansion. But Denmark, small and awkward, had been an irritant since 1848.

The essence of the problem was that the King of Denmark ruled, in addition to the Danish kingdom, the two so-called Elbe Duchies. Of these Schleswig, the more northerly, had a mixed Danish and German population, while Holstein and Lauenburg (a small state to the south of Holstein) were both German. Schleswig and Holstein had regarded themselves since the Middle Ages as indissolubly linked, and they had also been linked since then to the crown of Denmark. But Holstein was a member of the German Confederation; Schleswig was not. There were different laws of succession for the kingdom and the duchies. The Germans were in a majority in the two duchies, but in a minority in the kingdom of Denmark as a whole. In 1848 the German population of the duchies had risen against the King and aspired to an independent life under the Duke of Augustenburg. But the great powers intervened; Prussia, which had at first supported the rebels, thought better of it; the Frankfurt parliament, hoping for the prestige of success on this issue with a foreign state, had to see its hopes destroyed, and finally an international conference led to the treaty of London of May 1852, which Austria and Prussia, but not the Confederation, signed. The treaty provided for the eventual accession of Prince Christian of Glücksburg and called for a constitution which should weld the kingdom and the duchies together, but could not prevent Austria and Prussia from insisting that the two duchies should retain their separate legal identity, thus enabling them to frustrate all attempts by the King, Frederick VII, to produce the agreed constitution.

It was the death of King Frederick on 15 November 1863 that opened up new vistas for Bismarck. No doubt he saw in the question from the start the possibility of a success in foreign policy helpful to his position; but he was also lucky in the fact that the mistakes of others facilitated his plans. In March 1863 Frederick had incorporated Schleswig in the Danish state, and the Confederation had begun to make plans for the invasion of Holstein; Sweden had talked in July of coming to Denmark's assistance against a German attack, and Palmerston's famous statement in Parliament on 19 July 1863 that Denmark would not stand alone had apparently referred to the possibility of Swedish rather than British assistance. To solve the political deadlock the Danish Rigsraad had adopted a new constitution just before Frederick's death; his successor, Prince Christian of Glücksburg, gave his signature to this although it incorporated Schleswig in Denmark. This aroused the fierce but futile rage of the German liberals and the smaller

German states, which decided to recognize Prince
Frederick, the eldest son of the Duke of Augustenburg, as
ruler of the duchies. His cause was widely popular even in
Prussia, where he enjoyed the goodwill of both the King
and the Crown Prince. All Bismarck's moves are consistent with the view that he wished to frustrate the pretensions of the Augustenburgs at all costs; the likelihood that
the new state would look to Austria for support against
her powerful neighbour Prussia was sufficient reason for
this. At an early stage, however, the additional purpose
of annexing the two duchies to Prussia began to loom in
his mind as a possibility, although it was one that he was
careful not to avow. If this second aim were unattainable
it would appear that he preferred the restoration of
Danish rule through a 'personal union' under the Danish
crown, although this would have been considered an act
of gross disloyalty to the German Confederation and is
one which Bismarck's defenders among German historians strenuously deny.

Two events, however, favoured Bismarck from the start.
The first was the decision of the Austrian government on
24 November 1863 to work with Prussia in the Danish
question and to join her in advocating the maintenance
of the treaty of London of 1852. The other German states
were indignant but quite impotent when Austria and
Prussia united against them. The second was the decision
of Napoleon III, with whom Bismarck had been patiently
maintaining relations of vague goodwill, not to put himself forward as the opponent of German policy against
Denmark. These two developments were due partly of
course to the fact that Bismarck was profiting from the
care with which, in spite of his appearance of forceful-
ness, he had kept alternative doors open. But he was
helped by the shortsighted tactics of the others. Austria
with her own Polish problem in Galicia found France
critical and was tending to draw closer to Russia and
Prussia, while Rechberg was as opposed as Bismarck to
the pretensions of Augustenburg, but for the opposite
reason : *his* fear was that the prince would be forced to

make Schleswig–Holstein a Prussian satellite. Napoleon, knowing that Russia, Austria, and Britain were suspicious of his schemes and unfavourable to his dream of a great congress in Paris, saw in Prussia the only hope of a collaborator. And with Gorchakov and the Tsar persuaded that with all his oddities Bismarck was too useful to them to be lost, there was little but the undecided British cabinet to offer much trouble. But Bismarck rightly believed that Britain too was unlikely to do anything very violent.

Nevertheless during October and November 1863 he continued to urge the need for a peaceful solution, and it was only after Palmerston had rejected (with Austrian connivance) Napoleon's pet scheme for the great congress to settle the outstanding problems of Europe that he felt it safe to risk a more forcible interference. Faced with the astonishing spectacle of Austro–Prussian agreement the smaller German states lost their unity in the Confederation and agreed by a bare majority to accept the treaties as their ground for intervention in Holstein. To British remonstrances Bismarck took the line that he wanted nothing but the maintenance of the treaties—in short, the *status quo*—and advised stronger language on Britain's part to restrain the German Confederation. On 24 December Saxon and Hanoverian troops had entered Holstein and Lauenberg, but when they refused in January 1864 to advance into Schleswig, Prussian and Austrian troops did so instead. At the same time Prussian forces made themselves at home in Holstein with scant regard for the feelings of their Hanoverian colleagues, and when Saxony seemed inclined to press the claims of Augustenburg Bismarck mobilized an army corps on her frontier. King Christian's policy of no surrender made British intervention on his behalf difficult, and Bismarck was satisfied that only the installation of Augustenburg would bring this about. It suited him that the Danes should fight and so give Prussia the practical advantages of a military conquest, and while the subjugation of the Danish forces proceeded rapidly, he continued as long as possible to advocate the *status quo*. Austria remained tied

to her masterful ally and suffered in prestige among the
smaller German states in consequence. Inside Prussia
there were now the first signs of a movement of public
opinion in the government's favour.

But he was soon faced with the second and more difficult task of ending the crisis with the two duchies safely
in Prussian hands. On 3 February 1864, immediately
after the invasion of Schleswig, he first let the Prussian
crown council know that annexation was in his mind, and
he dropped sufficient hints to Rechberg to start the Austrians speculating as to the possibility of Italian gains for
themselves with Prussian backing as a reward for acquiescence in Prussian plans—which however they did not
much like. The French had to be squared in much the
same way. For some time the situation was a delicate one,
for consciences in Russia, France, and England were uneasy at Denmark's fate, and while military conquest had
its political advantages it was always possible that if it
went too fast or too far the others would intervene.
Accordingly Bismarck was not pleased when a Prussian
detachment crossed the frontier into Jutland on 18 February without authorization and seized the town of Kolding. This produced what was perhaps the most dangerous
moment for Prussia during the crisis. The British cabinet
contemplated a naval demonstration off Copenhagen on
21 February, and asked the French and Russians to adopt
a similar course. Napoleon III had already on the 20th
talked of co-operation with England, and in the French
press criticism of Prussia was mounting. Gorchakov
seemed to welcome the British plan.

But the moment passed : Austria denied that she intended to send men-of-war up the English Channel, Bismarck did his best to minimize the Kolding affair, there
was strong opposition from Queen Victoria and pacific
members of the British cabinet to the naval action, Napoleon changed his mind, and it was explained that the
Russian fleet would be ice-bound and immobile until mid-
May. The British cabinet decided on 23 February to post-
pone action, and its half-heartedness had already enabled

the Empress Eugénie to dissuade Napoleon from action. Bismarck was able during the following weeks to hold out the prospect of some unspecified gains for France—perhaps even the Rhine frontier—with Prussia's goodwill, and in the meantime the last of the Danish forces on the mainland were crushed. Victory at Düppel was the Prussian army's first for two generations. Hints that he might come to terms with France were sufficient to worry the British and Russian governments, and to leave them uneasy and inactive. He had all the cards in his hands when an international conference met in London on 20 April.

After this the fate of Denmark and the duchies was a matter for Prussia and Austria to settle between themselves, and it was to prove as incapable of a peaceful solution as the problems of the German Confederation, which also divided them and which had in no way been brought nearer to a solution by the Danish crisis. Balking at the prospect of a Prussian annexation, distrusting Bismarck's ready but unspecified offers of compensation elsewhere, the Austrians clung as long as possible to the plan for a personal union, but were defeated by the obstinate refusal of the King of Denmark to compromise. Rechberg then took the rather desperate course of proposing Augustenburg, and Bismarck, although certainly taken by surprise, joined him in proposing this to the conference on 28 May. The Danes would agree to nothing and were left to their fate. The conference accordingly broke up on 25 June; fighting began again, and on 12 July Denmark surrendered. Bismarck in the meantime had presented the Duke of Augustenburg with terms too onerous for him to accept. The international phase of the crisis ended on 30 October 1864, with the treaty of Vienna, by which the King of Denmark ceded his rights in Schleswig and Holstein unconditionally to Austria and Prussia.

From this point, the two duchies were important mainly as a field of manoeuvre for Bismarck in eliminating Austrian opposition to his plans for Germany. This is not to say that he was preparing only for war, although he had been regularly threatening it since 1862. He was developing an arrogant pride in his skill in manipulating political forces and a fierce dislike of surrendering the supreme control of events to others, and he was not a soldier. He had no Hitlerite or Napoleonic dreams of perpetual warfare, with one glorious campaign leading to another and yet another; for one thing, most of the glory would go to the Prussian general staff and not to him, and for another there is the curiously military quality of his diplomacy, which was quite enough to satisfy his fighting instincts and talent for manoeuvre. It was essentially a military approach in his use of threats, feints, alliance offers and demonstrations of force to jockey his slightly confused rivals out of one position after another. In such circumstances a bargain or promise was a *ruse de guerre* to be abandoned as soon as it had served its immediate purpose. He was quite ready to use war as an instrument of policy if necessary and convenient, but in the condition of Prussia and of his own government there were certain risks in doing so, and great difficulty (which called for a peculiar type of political skill) in getting the right war started at just the right time. He was clever and very cautious in keeping alternative courses open and we can trace this double planning and the reserving of decisions until the very eve of the final break with Austria. This did not rule out a preference or priority for one alternative, and we can say fairly definitely that after a certain point he was working for war. But the line of retreat was kept open to the last.

He was helped by the continued underrating of his ability and resources. Denmark was an insignificant military power, and some observers were not greatly impressed by the Prussian army's performance of its relatively simple tasks. The Austrians were thought to have shown more dash and spirit. 'The Prussian Army', wrote Lord Napier, the British ambassador at St. Petersburg, in April 1865, 'is far from perfect, the soldiers are ill-fed and ill-paid, the land defences of Prussia are incomplete, the railways of Prussia are in need of development and state assistance, the civil functionaries of Prussia are insufficiently remunerated.' In the political field many attributed such success as Bismarck had achieved to rough and desperate plunges assisted by luck. Napoleon based his calculations on the assumption that Prussia would probably get the worst of a clash with Austria. Others thought the same. Napoleon III was still considered Europe's master diplomatist, who would dupe the clumsy Prussian minister. It was Napier again who made a singularly ill-judged, but not unrepresentative, comment on the Biarritz meeting in October 1865. 'We can imagine the eccentric volubility with which M. de Bismarck would develop his sanguine schemes and the covert irony and silent amusement of the subtle sovereign.'

Moreover, the Danish affair had not ended the internal struggle in Prussia, although it had embarrassed the opposition and brought the government some popular support. At the end of 1863 the liberals were torn between their desire to keep company with the *Nationalverein* in subduing Denmark, and their distaste for any show of support for the Prussian cabinet. When Bismarck supported the London treaties instead of Augustenburg it seemed a confirmation of his indifference to the national cause. Benedikt Waldeck, the leader of the extreme radicals, was consistent in preferring the victory of parliament to the defeat of Denmark, and when Bismarck asked for a credit to support military action they opposed it. Such consistency was too much for the moderates, who somewhat awkwardly tried to dodge the accusation of mere obstruction by a resolution calling for a 'national policy' against Denmark. The government did not need the credit, and it is clear that Bismarck was merely putting them in the wrong. They fell into the trap when on 25 January 1864 they passed yet another resolution condemning the use of public funds without their authorization.

As the Prussian troops advanced, public enthusiasm grew, and a steady publicity campaign began to advocate a Prussian instead of a German solution, that is, Prussian annexation of the duchies instead of their rule by Augustenburg. By the end of 1864 the demand for annexation had powerful support, including that of the two historians, Treitschke and Mommsen. The liberal position was obviously weakening, but many had scruples about violating the principle of self-determination which they had recently been defending so vehemently. An increasing number of deputies were, however, wearying of the constitutional struggle, and at the beginning of 1865 Bismarck, with the prospect of the Austrian war before him, made another attempt at a settlement with the opposition on the basis of the military compromise of October 1862. King William again refused to yield anything of substance. So the deadlock continued, and the continued and ineffectual voting down by the liberal majority of money bills for Bismarck's increasingly popular plans merely strengthened their own sense of frustration.

In the meantime the official machine was regularly used to persecute and harass liberal candidates and voters. Hostile business firms were refused government contracts. Deputies were fined and imprisoned for criticizing the government. Many liberal judges were displaced, and civil servants disciplined. But still he preferred to leave the constitutional position as it was, in spite of serious talk in the cabinet of a return either to absolutism or to the universal suffrage of 1848. Of the two he preferred the second, but he was not yet sure of its effects.

He could count on the army, and on the uncompromising minister of war, von Roon. The King, whose conscience moved more quickly than his mind in the face of innovation, was the greatest problem, or so Bismarck was wont to claim in later years. Of the great powers Russia was uneasy at the prospect of an Austro–Prussian war because she feared the aggrandizement of France, and Great Britain felt much the same. Neither felt called on to intervene if the two despoilers of Denmark chose to quarrel among themselves, but both were sufficiently deceived by the Napoleonic façade to make some polite attempts to promote a peaceful solution. These did not trouble Bismarck, and in any case he had taken Napoleon's measure more successfully than the rest of Europe. There was no reason why he should not force the pace with Austria, although a peaceful abdication of her place in Germany would have been an enormous and adequate triumph.

So his problem was narrowing itself to that of ensuring either Austrian acquiescence in all his plans or a sufficiently defiant attitude on Austria's part to overcome King William's scruples about a fratricidal war, a war that is between German-speaking troops. On 22 August 1864, before the peace of Vienna, the two rulers and their foreign ministers met at Schönbrunn, and Bismarck was able to explore the first alternative. He appears to have offered rather vague assurances of support for Austrian policy in Italy in exchange for continued co-operation against the medium German states and Prussian annexation of the duchies. When Rechberg tried to tie the Prussians down to a precise bargain, however, Bismarck let the proposal die.

Rechberg's career died with it, for he had nothing to show as Austria's gains under the Prussian alliance; nothing came even of his last desperate attempt to secure a small success in the shape of a promise that the Austrian desire for membership of the *Zollverein* should be examined before 1872. At the time Bismarck was on holiday in France, and tended to leave economic questions to others, and particularly Rudolf von Delbrück, who said no; and Bismarck, who thought this nominal concession was worth making to keep the accommodating Rechberg in office, intervened too late to help him. Rechberg's resignation on 27 October 1864, as a result of both popular and official criticism, perhaps meant that the Austrian government was becoming more impatient for results; but there was nothing resembling a long term plan, and the Emperor was still loth to abandon the collaboration with Prussia. Moreover, Austria was too near bankruptcy to welcome foreign crises. The new foreign minister was

Count von Mensdorff, but he was a soldier with little diplomatic experience, and the more detailed handling of diplomatic business fell to Baron von Biegeleben, head of the German department of the Austrian Foreign Office. A more insistent tone now began to appear in despatches to Berlin, but it was still the Austrian aim to work with Prussia.

Bismarck treated the Austrian pressure and the Confederation's disapproval as the joining of a battle of wills and the struggle continued until, with some assistance from bellicose elements among the Austrian public, he was successful in goading the hesitant Austrian Emperor and foreign minister into war in 1866. The first crisis was at the end of 1864, when he demanded the withdrawal of the Confederate troops, Hanoverian and Saxon, from the duchies. As Austria and Prussia were now the sole rulers of the duchies this was difficult for Austria to oppose, but she pressed for the recognition of Augustenburg. In November Bismarck got his way to the extent of securing the diet's reluctant agreement to the withdrawal of the confederate troops and officials, but Austria continued to press for a solution of her own position and that of Prussia. If Prussia objected to Augustenburg, would she like to annex both duchies and give Austria compensation elsewhere, perhaps in certain areas of Württemberg and Silesia?

For about three months, in a rather maddening way, Bismarck would say neither yes nor no to these hints, but he made it clear that Augustenburg's appointment could be considered only in return for the granting of special rights to Prussia. When he at last defined these rights in February 1865 they amounted to a virtual annexation of the duchies, for they included Prussian control of the army and navy, Prussian occupation of key points, membership of the *Zollverein*, and the like. Austria refused to agree, and made a vigorous effort for some months to withstand the rapid Prussian steps to dominate Schleswig. The Augustenburg party was encouraged, and in the diet, with Austrian support, a resolution was carried in April

1865 calling on the two powers to hand over Holstein to Augustenburg. By this stage King William had accepted the idea of Prussian annexation, and when the diet's resolution was accompanied by a Prussian decision to transfer the chief Prussian naval station from Danzig to Kiel a breach seemed near.

It was Bismarck, however, who at this point advised against any hasty decision, and his deliberation has been variously explained. Since his whole conduct in the crisis shows remarkable ruthlessness at all essential points we can dismiss the idea of any sudden aversion for war, and there is nothing to suggest that he intended to give Austria any real concessions as the basis of an agreed solution. But there were greater stakes than Schleswig–Holstein to be considered, and the discussions really show no more than his ability to weigh the many contingencies rather more coolly than some of his colleagues. The issues were debated at the important crown council of 29 May 1865. It had been called by the King whose resolution was not quite sufficient for war but who did not wish to compromise. Bismarck was not yet sure that Austria had reached the end of her concessions, and he suggested two modifications in the February conditions which would still have left Prussia with the substance of control. This the King disliked, in spite of his hesitations about fighting Austria. It was partly to bring William to the point that Bismarck insisted that war depended on a 'free decision on the part of the King'. He spoke openly now of an Austro–Prussian war as one which would not be fought for the duchies alone, but to give Prussia a new relationship to the smaller German states. It also seems, however, that although von Moltke and von Roon were ready for war, Bismarck was not entirely satisfied about the financial position. And he had to complete his links with Italy and France.

So for a time he tested nerves in Vienna by angry complaints as to the offensiveness of the Augustenburg party, and then agreed in the convention of Gastein, concluded on 14 August 1865 and confirmed by William and Franz

Joseph on 20 August, to a new working arrangement with the Austrians. Under this plan the joint administration of the duchies came to an end; Holstein was in future to be administered by Austria, Schleswig by Prussia; the Emperor sold his rights in Lauenburg outright to the King of Prussia, and Prussia took possession of Kiel. King William gave pious thanks for a bloodless victory, and his ministers agreed to give Austria three months to show her true colours.

Lest the colours should not be of quite the right hue the Austrians in Holstein were steadily goaded into exasperation by General von Manteuffel, the Prussian governor of Schleswig, who on Bismarck's instructions made incessant complaints about their conduct. He had been appointed on the suggestion of Bismarck and Roon, who both desired to remove him from his immediate contact with the King. As the Gastein agreement had been treated in many quarters as a diplomatic defeat for Austria, further concessions by her were not easy, and she had put herself in a hopeless position by continuing the principle of joint sovereignty, which justified the Prussian interference. Bismarck was in an excellent position to stage-manage a rapid worsening of relations whenever he wished to do so. It must not be thought, however, that the Austrians were incapable of guile. Count Blome, the Austrian representative in Munich, who negotiated the agreement, believed that the duchies would be an embarrassment and a hostage to fortune for Prussia, just as Venetia was for Austria. And if Austria was criticized for the immorality of the partition, far more sweepingly in the Confederation was Prussia condemned as a ruthless exponent of power politics; this seemed to give Austria some cards to play. A further miscalculation by Blome and others in Vienna was the view that Bismarck was still concerned only in maintaining the conservative position in Prussia.

Bismarck's final problem in preparing for the decisive showdown with Austria was to ensure the non-intervention of France. Napoleon, like Franz Joseph, was following an ambitious course without the zest to push it to a warlike conclusion, and accordingly his role had insensibly become cautious and defensive. Franz Joseph was ready to conciliate Prussia, but could not give up his leadership of the Confederation; and Napoleon wished to be the arbiter of Europe but had no taste for war with either Austria or Prussia, if either should seek to upset the German balance of power. In practice, therefore, in spite of much mystification and talk of compensation, he had to accept what was coming to him and to Europe.

The immediate French reaction to the Gastein agreement was a sharp diplomatic note in which the French foreign minister, Drouyn de Lhuys, condemned it as having no other basis than force and the convenience of the two partners. But it was evidently the prospects of Austro–Prussian agreement which aroused French alarm. Bismarck hastened to reassure Napoleon through the French embassy that the Gastein agreement was only a stepping stone towards a final settlement with Vienna, and that after the annexation of the duchies and the completion of Prussian supremacy north of the Main, France herself could expand 'anywhere in the world where French is spoken'. He was able to see Napoleon at Biarritz early in October, and it appears that he did nothing to withdraw his hints and that Napoleon gave a guarded assurance that he was not proposing to side with Austria. But Napoleon was sickly and undecided, and not very forthcoming. He still regarded Austria, however, as the greater menace. Bismarck also hoped to enlist French pressure on the Italians, who had shown great coyness, during the period of the Gastein negotiations, towards his secret advances for an Italian–Prussian alliance against Austria. By the end of October 1865 he was probably satisfied that Austria, in spite of her attempt to woo France with commercial concessions, was isolated; but he had still to tie the Italians down and to ginger the King of Prussia up to a breach.

All the great powers were expecting an Austro–Prussian war after the beginning of 1866. The smell of powder was in the air. When the deputies of the German parliaments met in Frankfurt in October 1865 to condemn the Gastein treaty Bismarck had shown his annoyance by proposing that the dual powers should take steps to punish the free city for allowing such a meeting; in doing so he was undoubtedly indulging a personal irritation against the most celebrated home of German liberalism, but he was also seeking once again to commit Austria to a joint defiance of the liberal elements in the Confederation. But Mensdorff was unresponsive, and the Prussian press ominously critical of the 'half relationship' which this implied. Manteuffel's interferences in Holstein in the meantime exasperated the Austrians further, and helped the Augustenburg party, which held a demonstration at Altona on 23 January 1866. Bismarck's protest against the permission that had been given for the meeting was in menacing terms and was answered with some spirit by the Austrian government on 7 February, and Bismarck could now say that co-operation with Austria was at an end. Although the Prussian administration had done something to strengthen its popularity in Schleswig it was evident that his methods were having the reverse effect in Holstein. He rightly concluded that Austria was probably now at the end of her concessions, and that if so, war alone remained.

What was holding the Prussians back? It was still the King's troublesome conscience. Although he greeted each Austrian objection to Bismarck's provocative messages with splendid outbursts of indignation he still wanted to be finally persuaded that Austria was entirely in the wrong. But Mensdorff, although unable to surrender to threats, was still ready for some compromise settlement in the duchies, providing that Austria got something elsewhere, and that recriminations were avoided. All this was very trying to Bismarck's nerves, and in turn no doubt to those of his associates. The King did however go so far as to give his consent at a crown council on 28 February 1866 to the making of preparations for war, and Bismarck was able to conclude the alliance with Italy which seemed an indispensable means of splitting the Austrian forces. It called for some delicate manoeuvring on both sides, for neither trusted the other; but on 8 April Italy agreed to declare war on Austria if war broke out between Prussia and Austria in three months. King William's final agreement had still to be given.

The last stage of this strange, provocative political game was carried out successfully, and there can be no doubt that the Austrian government played into Bismarck's hands at certain points. It can also be said that until almost the last moment, with his extraordinary grasp of complicated events, he was keeping open an alternative course of action in case the solution by war became impossible through the King's final refusal to fight, or through some really serious threat of intervention by the other powers, or through Austrian concessions. But he was forced by the logic of his own aims and personality to seek war, for he knew that there was really no satisfactory bargain to be made with Austria. There could be no compromise over the duchies or surrender of Prussian territory in compensation, and it was equally impossible for him to contemplate anything short of the elimination of Austria from the Confederation. And yet he encouraged the efforts of Anton von Gablenz, brother of the Austrian governor-general of Holstein, to secure acceptance in Vienna and Berlin of a compromise plan, based on the division of Germany north and south of the Main into two military units, one commanded by Prussia and the other by Austria. The two duchies were to be independent, under a Hohenzollern prince, and subordinated to Prussia, with financial compensation to Austria, and backing for her interests in Italy. On 9 April Bismarck had put a quite different proposal to the Federal Diet for a German parliament based on universal suffrage, but this blatant bid for liberal support in the imminent war lost its dramatic effect when Austria and the medium states referred the matter to a committee for detailed examination. The Gablenz plan remained under discussion until the end of May, and Bismarck even

studied plans to amalgamate it with his proposal for a
national parliament.

The real immediate cause of war was the process of
mobilization. In March the Austrian government had felt it
necessary to take preliminary steps to mobilize against a
Prussian attack, for the process was always a slow one with
the Austrian forces. At the end of April Italian mobilization kept up the strain. For some weeks Mensdorff had
made a great diplomatic effort to persuade King William
to see reason; he pressed the British and Russian governments to make representations, and it was known that the
Crown Prince and Queen Augusta were critical of the
terrible chief minister. In the end Austria, who could not
bear the suspense and expense of mobilization for long,
took the initiative. On 1 June, in reply to the diet's demand for demobilization, she formally asked the diet to
find a solution of the Schleswig–Holstein question, thus
abandoning her treaty of January 1864 with Prussia, and
also the Gastein convention. This precipitate action,
which hurried on the war before the Austrian generals
were ready, was due to a proposal by Napoleon for a congress to settle outstanding European issues and to a somewhat panicky belief by the Austrian diplomats that they
must secure the support of the medium German states
quickly.

Bismarck could now call Austria a treaty-breaker; he
arranged for Manteuffel to march into Holstein, an action
which was followed by the withdrawal of the Austrian
forces there; and on 10 June the Prussian plenipotentiary
presented to the diet a proposal for the exclusion of
Austria from Germany. On the following day the Austrian delegate countered with a demand for the immediate mobilization of all the confederate forces against
Prussia. King William was at last convinced that his conscience allowed him to fight, and when the Diet agreed
to the Austrian proposal by nine votes to six on 14 June,
the Prussian reply was to declare the Confederation dissolved. Most of the confederate states remained neutral,
but hostile to Prussia. When ultimatums to Saxony, Han-

over, and Hesse-Kassel were rejected these states were invaded by Prussian troops. Both sides were very coy about declaring war, and it was only on 21 June, after declaring that a 'state of war' existed, that the Crown Prince crossed the Bohemian frontier with the advance troops.

The Prussians met with astonishing and rapid successes everywhere, while their Italian allies suffered equally spectacular defeat, on land and sea. The resistance of the forces of the three smaller states collapsed promptly, and the victorious Prussian columns entered Frankfurt. In Bohemia a competent Austrian general, Benedek, operating in unfamiliar territory with slow moving forces and inferior equipment, was defeated at the decisive battle of Sadowa or Koniggrätz on 3 July. The way to Vienna lay open, and Franz Joseph immediately sought Napoleon's intervention. So Bismarck had triumphed : the risks and the duplicity, the deliberate exposure of Prussia's future to the chances of battle, had been vindicated by the glamour of three weeks of continuous victory. In the process his diplomacy began to acquire subtleties in the eyes of many who had not hitherto observed them.

Chapter Three

From Confederation to Empire

IF Bismarck had died in the moment of victory at Sadowa, instead of watching the battle with grim satisfaction, clad in his grey uniform and steel helmet, from the comparative safety of the King's entourage, he would still have won a place of some importance in Prussian and European history. But his achievement would have been mainly one of destruction—of parliamentary government in Prussia, of the Confederation, of Austro–German friendship, and of the careers of a goodly number of his contemporaries, at home and abroad. The previous four years had been the anarchic or destructive phase of his career.

In unskilful hands the sequel to the victory might still have been disaster. The King and the generals might have plunged on to Vienna, perhaps incurring a French or even a Russian intervention, and a reconciliation with the sullen and timorous German medium states might have proved impossible. Prussia did not yet rule Germany or dominate the diplomacy of all Europe. But Bismarck was thinking furiously about all these problems, and the next five years constitute the second, and really constructive or creative, stage of his career. The third stage which followed during his long tenure of the Chancellorship of the German Empire (1871–1890) was essentially one of consolidation and defence.

His first task was to bring the war to a speedy end with a treaty of peace which secured for Prussia the maximum possible gains from her victory. The intervention of other governments in defence of the European balance of power seemed a serious possibility during July. France was the chief danger, although Russia became awkward at one point. Napoleon was highly embarrassed. He had counted on a long struggle. In his wretched state of health he had no zest for battle himself. Yet he felt he must assert himself. A wrong move on Prussia's part might have forced him to a military intervention, for although the French army was not ready for immediate war with the victorious and fully mobilized Prussians there was strong pressure from Drouyn de Lhuys, the French foreign minister, and the army leaders for the placing of an 'army of observation' on the Rhine.

Austria enabled Napoleon to pose as a mediator. On 4 July she asked him to arrange an immediate armistice with Italy in return for the cession of Venice, but as this was intended to enable Austria to continue the war by releasing her southern army he preferred to invite both Italy and Prussia to open peace negotiations immediately. Bismarck said later in his picturesque way that he thereupon swore a 'Hannibal's oath' that he would revenge himself on Napoleon in due course. But he showed no annoyance for the moment, and was ready to accept many of the conditions that Napoleon desired, such as that Austrian territory should remain intact, that the German Confederation should be limited to the area north of the river Main, and that the German states of south-west Germany should have an independent international existence.

The 'Hannibal's oath' nevertheless shows that he felt himself to be acting under duress; it puts the so-called leniency of his treatment of Austria in a somewhat less favourable light. Although he was opposed to the entry of King William and the Prussian army into Vienna he delayed the conclusion of the armistice while the Prussian forces moved deeper into Bohemia, and he had ready up to this point to use, if the need arose, a plan for the break-up of the Habsburg empire by inciting a Hungarian rising, a Serbian attack, Bohemian autonomy, and an advance of the Italian and Prussian army to Vienna. The

fact is that with his extraordinary knack of pursuing alternative objectives he had both the destruction of Austria
and her wooing into future alliance in mind. Only after
Austria had turned to France did he begin to insist that
'a further weakening of Austria by annexation of her
territory, must not take place, for we shall need her power
later for ourselves'.

During the next few days he negotiated over the terms
of peace with both the French government and, through
intermediaries, with the Austrians. His own view was that
he had done very well in securing French agreement to
his terms for Germany without being tied down to specific
plans for French compensation in German territory. He
agreed to the principle of independence for the south-west
German states and the integrity of Austrian territory, and
when he revealed on 18 July that Prussia's objective was
the annexation of 3 to 4 million inhabitants of north
Germany, Napoleon did not demur.

King William nevertheless was highly dissatisfied. He
had by now quite forgotten his conscientious scruples of
the previous two years over fratricidal war and the des-
poiling of his fellow rulers. Supported by the military, he
wanted some Bavarian and Austrian territory (in
Bohemia and Silesia), Schleswig and Holstein, and the
punishment of the hostile North German princes. The last
of these aims Bismarck secured through Napoleon's agreement to his plans for North Germany, but he had a hard
fight over his determination to avoid annexation of Austrian territory and the entry of Prussians into Vienna.
There were tears and recriminations. But with the Crown
Prince's unexpected help and a threat of resignation he
secured agreement to what the King bitterly described
as a shameful peace; Bismarck's sensitive feelings were
undoubtedly hurt by this silly grumble. But he was able
to conclude the armistice he wanted and the preliminaries
of peace at the Prussian headquarters at Nikolsburg on
26 July.

The terms were in accordance with the agreement
reached with Napoleon through the Prussian ambassador

in Paris, von der Goltz. But it had still to be seen whether they would be accepted without interference from the remaining powers. Napoleon and Drouyn de Lhuys still hankered after compensation. Although Gorchakov had been annoyed by Mensdorff's appeal to France alone for mediation he was eager for a European settlement which he might fashion and continue perhaps to preside over as a new Europe emerged from the revolutionary changes in Germany, Italy, and the Austrian Empire. On 27 July he proposed a European congress. But the British were unco-operative : the new British foreign secretary, Lord Stanley, thought the Nikolsburg terms moderate in the circumstances, and he believed at this stage that the peace of Europe was more likely to be endangered by the weakness than by the strength of Germany. Nevertheless, until the congress plan was scotched, Bismarck continued to beguile the hopeful Frenchmen. General Manteuffel, a respected figure, was sent to Russia to explain the need for Prussia's action.

It must be said that Napoleon's concern for the balance of power was not merely one of prestige; behind the uneasy search for compensation was a genuine anxiety over the defence of the French frontiers. In the power-vacuum of divided north Germany a new great power was about to be installed, and the French would have been foolish indeed not to be concerned over its strategical implications. Bismarck's tactic before the war and immediately after Sadowa was to give the impression that he recognized France's right to compensation, although he was careful to put nothing on paper, and there were frequent reservations as to Prussian public opinion and the King's stubborn aversion to the ceding of Prussian—but not perhaps of German—territory. It was necessary to keep the matter open now until at least the Russian idea of a congress had been dropped. On 13 July Napoleon had mentioned to Goltz that he wanted to acquire at least the fortress of Landau in the Palatinate. On 23 July he instructed the French ambassador to Berlin, Benedetti, to suggest that France should have the frontiers of

1814 and Luxembourg. Bismarck found time to talk expansively to Benedetti on 26 July and mentioned the Bavarian Palatinate and Belgium as very suitable acquisitions; but he could fairly say that at that moment, in the last stage of the Nikolsburg negotiations, he had no time to make detailed arrangements.

After the signing of the preliminary peace Napoleon was on somewhat weaker ground. But Benedetti was completely taken in by Bismarck's affability, and Drouyn was encouraged to propose a secret Franco–Prussian treaty giving France the Saar and territories belonging to Bavaria and Hesse-Darmstadt, with the withdrawal of the Prussian garrison rights in Luxembourg. Bismarck avoided a direct discussion of the details by denouncing the tone of the message as an ultimatum, and actually threatened war. Benedetti hurried back to Paris with his tail between his legs, Bismarck leaked some hints of the matter to the press, and Drouyn resigned. But after this the French merely put the matter in a milder form, limiting the proposal to Belgium and Luxembourg, and in mid-August Benedetti was so rash as to give Bismarck a copy of this proposal in his own handwriting. He heard no more about it until 1870, and Napoleon had gradually to recognize that he must regard the alliance project as dead.

The Russians were made of rather sterner stuff, and for a time Bismarck's threats to resist interference by proclaiming the constitution of 1849 merely caused irritation. But Manteuffel assured Gorchakov and the Tsar that Bismarck would stop at nothing, and on 13 August Gorchakov let the French ambassador know that Russia would not do anything further to interfere with the Prussian plans. On 23 August the treaty of Prague gave definitive form to the Nikolsburg agreement.

Bismarck had one further diplomatic corner to turn. The military operations against Austria's south German allies, Baden, Bavaria, Hesse-Darmstadt, and Württemberg, continued throughout July, with invariable Prussian victories against lukewarm opposition. He had no desire to leave these states to fall under the protection of either France or Austria, who were no doubt already speculating on the chance of securing them as allies through their fear of future Prussian encroachments. An armistice was concluded on 2 August, and it soon became clear that the four states, aided by the fact that they were asked to give up virtually none of their territory, were ready enough to make peace with their conqueror. Austria was a broken reed, and at the moment France, as Bismarck was able to show through his negotiations with Benedetti, had very real designs on German territory. Accordingly, Prussia's peace treaty with Württemberg in mid-August included a mutual guarantee of each other's possessions and also a secret article establishing an alliance between them and giving Prussia the control of Württemberg's armed forces in the event of war. Baden and Bavaria signed similar treaties. This was an extraordinary interpretation of his promise of complete independence for the states south of the Main. To add to the humour of the situation there was inserted in the treaty of Prague provision for the formation of a southern confederacy which would enjoy an independent international existence.

Let us now consider briefly the character of this complicated series of peace settlements. Austria gave up Venetia to Italy and her rights in Holstein to Prussia; she paid a light war indemnity; and she agreed to the dissolution of the German Confederation and to Prussia's right to assume the leadership in Germany. The treaty of Prague recognized the right of the German states south of the river Main to an independent existence. Bismarck has always been praised—it is the one point in his career which seems above criticism to admirers and critics alike —for the moderation shown towards Austria in these terms. Even Erich Eyck, by no means a friendly critic, calls it one of the surest and best foundations of his enduring fame. Heinrich Friedjung, the most eminent Austrian historian of the crisis, also believed that Bismarck was aiming at a genuine reconciliation with Austria and the southern states, although he remarked later that it was natural that the war left a feeling of bitterness in Austria and a desire for revenge. This is a point that Bismarck's admirers tend to forget : his peace policy did not, in itself, conciliate Austria. And it certainly pleased no one else outside Prussia.

The fact is that the peace settlement appears more lenient to our generation than it did in 1866, owing partly to a misreading of the situation at the time. It was no more 'lenient' than the general run of mid-19th century peace treaties—such as those of 1829, 1856, and 1859. In all these the defeated power gave up some territory, but was not basically weakened. And Bismarck was not in a very good position to demand more, even if he had wanted it.

The victor in any war, if he has any sense, always tries to avoid mere violence and plunder, and asks himself what his future relations with the defeated power are likely to be. If the defeated power is not of great potential military strength but is a possible future ally of his enemies he may think it best to take the risk of a lenient treaty; if it is very weak (as were the small north German states) he can be heavy-handed with impunity; if it is potentially strong enough to seek revenge he is faced with a much more complex problem. Should he risk conciliation, thus giving the enemy the chance of a comeback? Or should he try to crush him for a long time ahead? There is a sense in which Bismarck inclined to the first course with Austria, and the third with France in 1871, but in fact both aspects were present in some measure in both cases.

It does not look much like a lenient treaty when we count up the gains which filled so many of Bismarck's fellow countrymen with jubilation. Austria had been driven out of Germany, thus losing a struggle which had commenced with Frederick the Great (or even the Emperor Maximilian). If Austrian territory was not annexed, Schleswig and Holstein virtually were, and four German states—Hanover, Hesse-Kassel, Nassau, and

Frankfurt—were annexed to Prussia outright. He had
wanted to take all Saxony, and had given up this aim
reluctantly, owing to Austria's stout defence of her ally.
All the defeated paid indemnities. Frankfurt was treated
brutally; an enormous fine was imposed on Bismarck's
orders, starvation threatened as a means of hastening payment, and only after the burgomaster had hanged himself in despair was Bismarck again thwarted in some
measure by the procrastination of the senate and the
intervention of Queen Augusta. Some four and a half million persons had been added to Prussia's existing 19 millions. Nor can it be assumed that the annexed always
welcomed their fate. In Hanover, after the King, George
V, had been deposed, a strong opposition party formed
itself in his support. As a result the interest from the
King's fortune was seized by the Prussian government on
3 March 1868, just after an agreement to hand it over
to him had been signed. These so-called Guelph funds
(*Welfen-Fonds*) were invaluable to Bismarck henceforth
for many secret activities, including subventions to the
press.

Much good sense and very little good will, tremendous
determination allied to a wonderful grasp of political
possibilities, the sensitiveness but also the objectivity of an
artist, a lust for success, the driving force of a nervous
system infuriated by personal rebuffs, and the precious
gift of a really good brain from the Prussian God whose
intentions he understood so well—all these qualities he
had in abundance, but he was incapable of magnanimity.
He had been very successful up to this point. This led
critics and admirers to exaggerate the uniqueness of his
personality, but it is not necessarily to regard him as more
brutal or more unscrupulous, or more heroic or courageous, than other national leaders of his day in Europe.
He merely had better judgment, better tactics, and—at
the great moments of crisis—better nerves.

The second task which faced him immediately after
completing the international phase of the settlement was

that of establishing passable working relations with the many Prussian and north German politicians over whom he had recently triumphed so completely. He had to ensure Prussia's domination of the North German Confederation but at the same time to create some genuine goodwill towards her ascendancy. He was to show on the whole remarkable affability and tact in handling everyone concerned with the negotiations. This ability to resort to an almost conspiratorial geniality when the need arose was well illustrated in August and September in his negotiations with the rulers of the surviving independent states north of the Main, although he was now on the verge of collapse with pain, depression, and insomnia. The alliances that he concluded with fifteen of the former on 18 August provided the ground plan of the Confederation. They retained their territories, and agreed that a constituent assembly based on direct manhood suffrage should be summoned to devise a constitution. These were for the most part the smaller fry among German states —such as Anhalt, Brunswick, Saxe-Weimar, Saxe-Altenburg, Saxe-Coburg-Gotha, Waldeck, Schaumburg-Lippe, Bremen, Hamburg, and Lübeck—and to them were added Mecklenburg on 21 August and Saxony on 21 October. At the same time he was sufficiently conciliatory towards the discomforted Prussian liberals to lay the foundation of an enduring alliance.

The four-years' defiance of the Lower House seemed to have ended in complete victory for the government when Sadowa was won and polling in a general election, begun on the same day (3 July), led to substantial gains for the Conservatives and a serious setback for Bismarck's opponents, the Progressives. The figures were : Conservatives 142 deputies, Progressives 85, Left Centre 65, Old Liberals 26, Poles 21, Centre 15. Bismarck again upset the King and baffled his glum Conservative friends by what seemed to them an unnecessary and uncharacteristic disinclination to press home his full advantage. But in fact he had, as we have seen, tried more than once since taking office in 1862 to settle this dispute to his own advantage.

The bargain that he was prepared to offer was an acceptance of some Liberal procedures in return for his enjoyment of the reality of power, particularly with regard to foreign affairs and war.

The Liberals were too limited in their objectives, and too dedicated to the pursuit of national greatness, to be able to struggle on with much heart in a cause which had so clearly been based on a misreading of the facts; for they could no longer assume either that the electorate was behind them or that the King, Bismarck, and the army could not get on without them. In the circumstances, asked some of the more hardbitten ministers, why apologize to them? The uses of a co-operative Liberal group in the next phase of the political struggle were, however, obvious enough to Bismarck and he seems to have found some amusement in affable, tactful discussions during August leading towards an acceptable compromise. It took the form of an indemnity bill, which meant that in agreeing to pardon the government's breaches of the constitution the opposition would secure an admission that a breach had taken place.

On the other hand the King gave no guarantee, as he publicly observed to everyone's embarrassment, that he would not act in the same way again. All that could be said was that the formal right of the Prussian parliament to initiate money bills had been reasserted, with no more likelihood than in the past four years that it could be enforced. The bill passed on 3 September by 230 votes to 75. It shattered the Progressive party; the majority who voted for the bill formed themselves in due course into the 'National Liberal' party, the main support of Bismarck's policies for the next twelve years. To this group, which already included such prominent or rising figures as Max von Forckenbeck, Karl Twesten, and Hans Viktor von Unruh, were to be added most of the liberal leaders in the recently annexed states. These included Rudolf von Bennigsen and Johannes Miquel from Hanover.

At this point the accumulated physical and emotional

tensions of the last months had their effect, and Bismarck
was found to be suffering from a return of the digestive-
rheumatic trouble which had caused the first break in his
youthful record of robust health in 1859. He was away
from Berlin from the end of September until the beginning of December 1866. Apparently the bout was severe,
and his wife, a devoted and rigorous nurse, cut him off
from all mental toil and official correspondence. The convalescence was spent on a pleasant estate on the island of
Rügen, attended by his daughter Marie as well as his
wife. That this rather long absence from the capital in
no way weakened his political authority is evidence of an
ascendancy which was to be illustrated by even longer
absences, usually with less excuse, during the next twenty-
five years. He could also, in spite of his wife's attempt to
stop it, allow his mind to ponder the next major problem
—the consolidation of the North German Confederacy.

And so the way was clear for a further task, the con-
summation of Prussian predominance in the new federal
north German state. It is typical of Bismarck's peculiar
brand of political realism that while we know a great deal
about his plans and ideas for the new constitution and the
effective concentration of power we find little evidence
of any thinking about the new state's mission or purpose
in the world. The state, like so much in German phil-
osophy and endeavour, was an end in itself; the use to
which it should be put, and to which it would put itself,
had still to be defined. National ambitions and policies—
economic, colonial, militaristic—were for the most part
the result and not the cause of union; and usually because the creation of power brought with it a swelling
pride and a desire to demonstrate its might, the German
nationalist became an expansionist and at the same time
a victim of fears as to the jealousy of his neighbours. Bismarck had talked of a future need for Austria, and the
threat from France was obvious enough. But this was
essentially a projection of his immediate preoccupation
with North German consolidation. He had no particular

ideas about building up a great industrial state, certainly no plans for Napoleonic conquests, no dream of a colonial empire, and no divine call to make Germany safe for liberalism and(or) democracy. He bent his whole efforts to the immediate work ahead.

Some historians have also found difficulty in deciding exactly what he was aiming at in terms of German unification. He can be quoted (sometimes out of context) as a contemptuous critic of the movement for national unity, arguing that the loyalty of the majority of Germans was to their dynasties rather than to the nation. He also talked about 'the German swindle'. But as he had been talking repeatedly since 1858 of the political advantages of an appeal to German nationalist sentiment we must take it that he knew it as something that existed and could be turned to political account, even if it involved a somewhat superficial or artificially-induced enthusiasm. The two loyalties need not conflict. If they showed a likelihood of doing so in one of the assimilated states the clash might be avoided either by persuading the ruler to co-operate with Prussia lest worst befall, or by presenting the nationalist issue so as to turn the emotions of the ruler's subjects against him. Three things are quite clear. Having fought the war in order to destroy Austrian predominance in the old federation, he did not intend that any basis of authority should exist in the new one other than that of Prussia; he had no desire to bring Austria in again, and therefore he was satisfied with a *kleindeutsch* position; and he intended to bring in the south-western group as soon as possible. It went without saying that the constitutional structure was shaped to ensure his own preponderance as far as possible.

According to a picturesque story, which has its place in the Bismarckian hagiology, he drafted the whole constitution single-handed in a couple of days after his return to Berlin, completing it on 9 December 1866. Like all such documents it was the work of many hands, but it was his brain child in the sense that it had its origin in his proposal to the diet at Frankfurt on 10 June 1866. Since

then drafts had been prepared by various persons including Savigny and Max Duncker, and by the ministries of
war and commerce, and it was this material that he now
shaped, with the help of Lothar Bucher, into a form
which suited his own ideas. This meant the taking over of
the outward form of the old Confederation with on the
one hand certain features intended to advertise and popu-
larize its national character and on the other a machinery
of government which put power even more firmly into
the hands of the King of Prussia and his chief minister
than had been the case under the Prussian constitution of
1850. It might be said to have contained something for
everybody, but not quite enough for Bismarck to secure
the acceptance of his own draft without modifications.
On the other hand the conflict of interests enabled him
to divide and threaten his critics, and to get his way on
the substantial points. Undoubtedly this was an example
of masterly political manoeuvring.

According to Bismarck's draft the various states included in the new federation were to retain control over
their internal affairs, but the president of the Confederation was to be responsible for foreign affairs, with the
right to conduct diplomatic negotiations, conclude treaties, and to declare war. There was to be a confederate
army, to which the states would supply contingents, but
while the princes would be the chiefs of their state contingents and could use the troops for police and similar
purposes within their own borders, the army as a whole
was to be under the personal command of the King of
Prussia. To retain as far as possible the outward form of
the old Confederation there was to be, according to Bismarck's draft, a President and a Bundestag as before. The
President was to be the King of Prussia. The Bundestag
was soon renamed 'Bundesrat' because of the Crown
Prince's objection to the old terminology. It was similar
to the former federal Diet, and consisted of representatives of the state governments, who were to vote according
to their governments' instructions. This body was not the
upper house of a parliamentary system but was more

akin to a cabinet or privy council; the members had ministerial status, and were to be responsible through committees for various branches of the public administration. A minister called a Chancellor would preside over the Bundesrat.

There was finally to be a Reichstag or parliament, elected by universal manhood suffrage. This indeed seemed a thoroughly democratic innovation. But the new parliament was in no sense an instrument for providing responsible government. It was to have no control over the Bundesrat. It would have the power to legislate on various matters, but to become law each bill would have to be approved by the Bundesrat. Moreover in Bismarck's original plan the main item of federal expenditure, the maintenance of the armed forces, was virtually taken out of the hands of the Reichstag by the provision that the size of the army and the amount that it was to cost per head were to be permanently fixed at an agreed percentage, after which the Reichstag would have merely the function of passing the military budget annually without any scope for modification. As Erich Eyck has rightly pointed out, political life in Germany would have come to an end if this final draft had become law. When Bismarck's draft was presented to a council of ministers representing the states nearly all disliked it. He saw the need for tactical concessions, although the rivalry between the various interests involved enabled him to play one off against the other. He could always threaten an appeal to the Reichstag elected by universal suffrage, which was to approve the new constitution; by these means he was able to defeat a proposal by Oldenburg for a hereditary Kaiser (instead of a president), a confederate cabinet, and a chamber of princes. This was essentially an attempt to weaken Prussia's predominant position by creating a genuine central government.

This made it all the more necessary, however, for him to carry the majority of the Reichstag with him. Here his newly won links with the National Liberals proved of decisive value. As far as possible he saw to it that they were not obstructed at the elections, as in the past, by Prussian officials. The masses responded to Bismarck's confidence in their judgment by electing deputies almost exclusively of wealth and rank; nearly half were noblemen, and the largest party were the National Liberals with 79 seats, while the Conservatives gained 59, the free Conservatives 39, the Old Liberals 27, and the Progressives only 19. The remainder of the 297 deputies included unqualified opponents, mainly Poles, Danes, Schleswig-Holsteiners, and the like. Outside these small groups, however, only the Progressives were strongly hostile and uncompromisingly insistent on responsible government and full parliamentary control of the budget. The National Liberals were prepared to temper their liberalism in the Prussian interest, but were rather active in pressing Bismarck as far as he was prepared to go in concessions to their principles. In this they were moved less by doctrinaire impulses than by the conviction that unless they could show that the German parliament had some life and authority of its own they could not hope to commend the Confederation to the German brethren south of the Main. Bismarck, who was clearly well aware that it would be expedient to disguise the naked reality of Prussian militarism as much as possible, did recede to some extent from his first uncompromising plans. The constitution was nevertheless the subject of some fierce debating between 24 February and 16 April 1867.

There were changes of some magnitude as a result. The most important concerned the military arrangements known as the 'iron budget'. There was strong dislike even among the National Liberals of the plan for fixing the annual payment and the intake of conscripts in perpetuity, and at first Bismarck seems to have been prepared to ignore the Reichstag and impose this arrangement by force. He made a famous speech on 11 March 1867, asking how a soldier invalided home from Sadowa would like to hear that nothing had been won except the right to put the existence of the Prussian army in question every year. 'Gentlemen, this situation is impossible!' he exclaimed. And he ended with an appeal. 'Let us set Germany in the saddle. She will be able to ride all right.' However, his hearers were not convinced, and finally Bismarck agreed to Forckenbeck's proposal that the arrangement should operate only until 31 December 1871, when it could be re-examined.

Bismarck had no apparent objection to a number of proposals which were designed to strengthen the legislative powers of the confederation; it seems that he had dealt sketchily with these matters in his draft in order not to ruffle the states too much, but he knew that there would have to be a growth of the central legislative authority as time went on. But he was adamant in refusing a proposal by Bennigsen that all the future ministers should countersign the presidential orders in their spheres of government. The effect of this refusal was to make the chancellor a very important figure, and Bismarck, who at first seems to have thought of the foreign minister as the key figure, had evidently decided by this stage to assume the office of chancellor himself. He reluctantly agreed to the secret ballot in place of open voting; hitherto he had been curiously insistent that secrecy was in contradiction to the 'best qualities of the German blood'. However, the liberal deputies were thinking apprehensively of Napoleon's manipulation of the mass vote with the sheeplike proletariat driven to the polls. He did insist on the non-payment of members, in order that the deputies at least would come from a class which had property to preserve. The Progressives had to accept the defeat of a proposal to include in the constitution a bill of rights, an unusual omission from written constitutions. With these final decisions the battle ended, and the constitution as amended was passed by 230 votes to 53 on 16 April 1867. On 31 May it was accepted by the Prussian Landtag by 227 votes to 93; in both cases the minority, consisting mainly of the Progressives, Catholics, and Poles, was largely the same.

Bismarck's liberal critics had every right to complain. A thinly disguised authoritarianism had been imposed on the Confederation. He would rule Germany as Chancellor, subject to the approval of his master, the King of Prussia; and the King could be managed. He hated the sharing of power; and while he no doubt told himself that it was in the best interests of Prussia, with great tasks ahead, that his hands should be free, he was determined to have his own way, whether there were compelling reasons of state or not. The trouble with this arrangement was that no one man could be equally expert in all the arts and departments of government, and even if he were he would have to retire sooner or later; the tasks which the exceptional man with astonishing tenacity and virtuosity could handle singlehanded for some years would almost certainly be too much for a successor of more ordinary mould. Nor under this system could successors be easily trained. The refusal to share power with any competing authority except the King meant in turn that the political education of the German people was stultified. Spengler wrote many years later that Bismarck's great flaw, as compared with Frederick William I, was that he could achieve, but could not form, a tradition. 'He did not parallel Moltke's officer corps by a corresponding race of politicians who would identify themselves in feeling with his State and its new tasks, would constantly take up good men from below and so provide for the continuance of the Bismarckian action-pulse for ever.' When he did begin to groom a successor in the eighties it was his son Herbert.

Thus the struggle against disunity was taking a form which, by facilitating one man's work, perpetuated disunity elsewhere. The basic arrangements under the constitution of the North German Confederation were, as we shall see, continued in the constitution of the Empire in 1871. One result was to assure the ultimate autocracy of the King of Prussia, whose power to make suicidal decisions remained; Bismarck's superb political judgment and psychological dominance saved the King from these, and then handed on the privilege unimpaired to his successors.

The iron budget and the masterful way in which Bismarck took charge of everything also prevented any democratic control of the army; its authority and arrangements were almost completely removed from any form of parliamentary control, and partly, in view of the King's personal responsibility for the army, from Bismarck's control too. He had already had brushes with the military cabinet between 1862 and 1866. During the Austro–Prussian war there had been further clashes with the military chiefs, who strove to keep both him and von Roon in ignorance of operational matters and who also tried at times to make diplomacy dependent on their views of military needs. The Prussian ministry of war was officially responsible for the administration of the confederate army, but in practice the military cabinet, now under Hermann von Tresckow, steadily increased its independent authority. The general staff, dominated by its successful chief Helmuth von Moltke, was also growing in importance and tending to free itself of the control of the ministry of war. Bismarck was to experience further clashes with von Moltke during the Franco–Prussian war.

The sense of crisis continued after 1866; it was genuine, widespread, and probably unnecessary, for no one really seriously proposed to upset the new arrangements. Bismarck was already turning over in his mind ways of bringing in the south-western states, and France might impede these plans; or she might give an excuse for another swift victory by the army and so provide the emotional setting for the completion of unification. He proceeded with the same mixture of non-committal frankness and provocative obstinacy which had lured Austria to her doom in 1866.

And yet, if Europe hovered on the edge of a major crisis for some time, it was through no particular initiative on his part. To embark on another major war so soon after the last, and when the North German Confederation was still being shaped, would have been difficult and confusing. Prussia's advance had evidently created widespread alarm and little sympathy abroad. Just as Napoleon's attitude had driven the south German states towards Prussia, so Belgium, Holland, and Luxembourg were shaken by the territorial ambitions of Prussia, and looked to France and more remotely to England for protection.

After his rebuff in August 1866 Napoleon felt that Luxembourg was the minimum that would satisfy his itch for compensation, and negotiations for the transfer of the duchy to France went on during the winter. This might be the Danish situation over again : for the duchy came under the personal rule of the King of Holland, but had been joined to the German Confederation in 1839. While the Confederation was now dissolved, the Prussian garrison remained. But when the King of Holland agreed on 19 March 1867 to sell the duchy to France for five million gulden, Bismarck seemed acquiescent, and even suggested privately that some pro-French demonstrations by the leading citizens of Luxembourg would facilitate the withdrawal of the Prussian garrison.

Although he had no desire to do Napoleon a service he would probably have accepted the situation if the transfer had been put through speedily and smoothly. But the moment for this had already passed. With the critical debates on the constitution approaching he could not afford to have any aspersions cast on his nationalistic fervour. He chose this moment to publish the texts of the treaties of alliance with the south German states in order to show that he had not left them to the mercy of Napoleon; the news came as a further dreadful rebuff to the French government. The French also overdid the anti-Prussian demonstrations in Luxembourg, and there was a press storm in Prussia against the cession. The temptation to strike an attitude was too great, and when Bennigsen hurled a pre-arranged interpellation about the duchy at Bismarck in the Reichstag on 1 April, he promised to maintain all German rights, while striving for a solution honourable to all parties. Yet he was not seeking war with France; he contemplated a bargain involving French agreement to the annexation of all Schleswig in return for the abandonment of Luxembourg, and Stanley made it abundantly clear that he saw no objection to some small satisfaction for the French. A solution of sorts was found in a conference in London which provided on 9 May 1867 for the neutralization of the duchy and the withdrawal of the Prussian garrison. This was Napoleon's solitary *pourboire* after all his talk of compensation.

The result was not popular in Germany. Moltke thought that France would have to be fought, and that it was better not to wait. But Bismarck seemed satisfied enough with the position. At the international exhibition in Paris, which he visited in June 1867 with Moltke and the King, he was in a genial mood, accepting with amusement some hisses from the crowds, and thoroughly enjoying the dances, banquets, parades, and sightseeing in a city which after all he knew well. The virtual collapse of Gorchakov's hopes of an agreement with France no doubt added to his good humour.

This last fact was, all the same, a reminder of the extremely uncertain state of the European balance, and of Prussia's virtual isolation. While the Luxembourg crisis had familiarized the government in every European capital with the likelihood of an early Franco–Prussian war, it had revealed no sympathy in any quarter with Prussian aspirations. In the four southern states there was evident apprehension in some quarters that they would be dragged into war merely to further Prussian ambitions. France, if she was to be fought, must be isolated, and this meant that as far as possible she must be left, with her ineffectual dynamism, to discredit herself; the problem was the reverse of that which had been posed by his relations with Austria, a lymphatic entity which had needed to be assisted into compromising situations.

So on the whole the later sixties saw very little positive diplomatic activity on Bismarck's part. While he waited for the international situation to take a more favourable turn there was much to be done at home. His interest in the details of legislation and commercial negotiations was fitful, but the admirable Prussian officials and the well-trained bureaucratic regime went ahead with the elaboration of the governmental structure of the new state. He felt able to spend longer periods away from Berlin, and his health improved. The chamber of deputies had voted rewards to the successful generals with Bismarck's name at the head of the list; the handsome donation of 400,000 thalers (£60,000) which he received enabled him to buy a heavily wooded estate at Varzin in Pomerania, far from the madding crowd but not from the courier and the post office. He would disappear for months to this Junker haven.

An improvement in the diplomatic situation did not come until the spring of 1868, and it was the result of events in Turkey rather than in western Europe. A rising in Crete and revolutionary rumblings in the Balkans tempted Gorchakov to speculate on the possibility of a major revision of the 1856 treaties to parallel the major changes that Prussia had introduced into central Europe. He sought the collaboration of Britain, France, and Austria to this end, in each case without response. The British were quietly but steadily pro-Turkish, and whatever their aversion to intervention in central Europe they had no intention of abandoning Turkey without a struggle. Feelers in Paris after September 1866 found the French evasive; desperate for a successful role in foreign affairs, they were more inclined to seek it in the Near East in defence of Turkey and in furtherance of reform. There were signs that Austria would seek compensation for her rebuffs in Italy and Germany by a more active Balkan policy, perhaps supporting Catholic propaganda in the peninsula, and this was not likely to be to Russia's advantage. Friendly Austrian approaches to the Poles were also alarming. So Russo–Austrian relations were again very cool during 1867. Prussia alone was making no attempt to put a spoke in Russia's wheel.

For Bismarck too the drawing together of Britain, France, and Austria was worrying. With the former Saxon diplomat, Baron Friedrich Beust, in authority in Vienna the ostensible Austrian plan was to prepare for a war of revenge, and the British had shown no disposition to share Bismarck's crocodile tears over the Germanic character of Luxembourg. His unequivocal assurances that Prussia had no axe to grind in the Balkans gave Russia some negative encouragement; closer co-operation was clearly necessary for both governments. So there came about the firm Russo–Prussian understanding which made the war of 1870 possible, and perhaps inevitable. The negotiations are characterized by Bismarck's easy skill in securing the maximum of advantage with the minimum of commitment; he responded warmly but somewhat vaguely to Gorchakov's first approaches, and dodged a hint that Prussia should oppose an Austrian seizure of Bosnia. On 20 March 1868 Gorchakov offered to place 100,000 men on the frontier to prevent Austrian aid to France in a Franco–Prussian war. Bismarck and King William were content with an unwritten affirmation of the principle of mutual assistance, to operate if either were attacked by two other great powers. Gorchakov was satisfied, although he would have liked more. This was a very adroit piece of diplomacy on Bismarck's part.

But in the meantime plans for strengthening the Confederation were not going at all well. The Luxembourg crisis had not generated sufficient passion to drown southern particularism in a new patriotic flood. The four southern states were reminded of all they distrusted in Prussian policy when they examined the new constitution. Those who wanted to combine federalism with the essentials of particularism were unwilling to be dominated by Prussia. This feeling was strongest at first in governing circles in Bavaria, Hesse, and Württemberg, but soon the liberals in each of these states became conscious again of the dilemma of liberal nationalism. Baden was a refreshing exception, for the Grand Duke and his ministers had the support of the strongest party, the Progressives, in favouring German unity. But Bismarck did not think it desirable for Baden to come into the Confederation alone.

He had hopes for a time of the *Zollparlament*. The changes in 1866 had made the existing *Zollverein* treaties out of date, and the peace treaties had provided for their revision. Bavarian opposition in March 1867 defeated his suggestion that southern representatives should join the Reichstag for the discussion of commercial and tariff questions. However, the economy of the southern states compelled them to stay in the *Zollverein*, and they agreed in July 1867 to Bismarck's alternative plan for a central body to discuss *Zollverein* matters. Bavarian influence was again decisive in securing the strict limitation of the discussion to the tariff question and certain fields of taxation. More than half the deputies elected to this *Zollparlament* by the four states were dedicated particularists who were determined to frustrate any attempts to widen its scope. Bismarck soon recognized the uselessness of any such plans, and left the business mainly in the hands of Rudolf von Delbrück, head of the *Bund* chancery.

Sentiment fluctuated in each of the four states for and against accession to the Confederation, but even the attempt to form a separate southern Confederation was defeated. Prince Hohenlohe, the prime minister of Bavaria, put forward a modest plan for a loose and limited southern union at the end of 1867. Bismarck welcomed it, much to the surprise of some of the southern ministers, in the hope that it would pave the way to incorporation in the northern unity. Particularist feeling in Bavaria and Württemberg killed the plan in 1868. On the other hand the four states showed no desire to link up with Austria or France against the North German Confederation, and their armies were being steadily permeated by Prussian influence and methods—partly through nationalist feeling, partly through recognition of the vast superiority of Prussian efficiency and technique. But something further was needed to galvanize nationalist sentiment and swing southern opinion in favour of unity; and Bismarck had found no means of peaceful inducement.

Meanwhile von Moltke and the generals were putting the finishing touches to their strictly academic plans for a war with France, to meet any hypothetical crisis that might arise. Everyone knew that a war with France was possible; what was less clear was that it had become the sole means of generating the great force of nationalist emotion which would complete the union. This is not to say, however, that Bismarck simply picked a quarrel in his own time. The position was rather that, with no theoretical objection to war, and with a clear understanding of the pros and cons of a number of alternative courses, he was still waiting to see how the French would adjust themselves to the new German situation. Napoleon's problem was to find some escape from his dreadful dilemma following the Luxembourg crisis, which had shown Bismarck's extremely grudging attitude to all forms of 'compensation'. Even if things stayed as they were in Germany Napoleon needed some face-saving success, although not necessarily at Germany's expense.

So plans for a Franco–Belgian customs union were pursued for a time, but had a setback in 1869; Bismarck did not interfere, but he thought it worthwhile to hint in London that Belgian independence was threatened. Army reform had been canvassed since 1866, but the French Chamber rejected universal service on the Prussian model, and only after much publicity was a more limited scheme agreed to in February 1868. French discussions with Austria turned, as the Russo–Prussian discussion had done, on a war involving Austria and Russia as well as on one involving Prussia and France, but in spite of much talk about contingent help and moral support a draft Austro–French treaty of 10 May 1869 remained unsigned. Both powers hoped to draw Italy into a triple alliance, but the Italian government first raised its terms and then insisted on the evacuation of French troops from Rome as the *sine qua non* of an agreement. After the French elections of 23 and 24 May 1869 had given the government only a bare majority there was something like an interregnum for six months, with the Chambers prorogued and Napoleon himself prostrated with illness; then in December 1869 he called on the leader of the opposition, Émile Ollivier, to form a government, and it was a question of waiting to see whether this would mean the salvation of the monarchy by means of domestic reforms and a policy of peace.

Anyone who followed French developments as closely as Bismarck knew that it would take very little to enrage the French press and many sections of public opinion and wring from the government party, known as *Arcadiens* or *Mameluks*, demands for vigorous foreign action. He told Moritz Busch in February 1870 that the Arcadians were waiting their opportunity, but that Napoleon was at the moment well disposed towards Germany; nothing should be done which might endanger the constitutional evolution of France, 'an evolution hitherto promoted in every way from Berlin, as it signifies peace for us'. This, however, clearly refers only to the immediate situation; it did not imply a belief that any French government would be able to acquiesce in the completion of the German union. The courses open to Bismarck were therefore to wait, possibly for years, until southern nationalists gained the upper hand and declared for union, or to hasten matters by precipitating some crisis with France which would swing southern opinion more quickly. If he followed the first course it might still happen that France would interfere. Against the view that he was following the second course there can be quoted a number of statements such as that made to Busch; he had told the German minister in Munich, Werthern, on 26 February 1869, that arbitrary interference in the course of history has never had any other result than the shaking down of unripe fruit, which German unity obviously was at the moment.

However, this only meant that the fruit was unripe in February 1869. There were a number of reasons for forcing matters in the spring of 1870. When he had been compelled to refuse Baden's entry into the North German Confederation in February he had been attacked by the

National Liberal deputy Eduard Lasker for indifference to the cause of unity, an accusation which seemed to be supported by his friendly attitude towards the idea of a southern confederation. Reichstag elections were due later in the year, and after them the iron budget would not be safe without a heightened sense of external crisis. Since the beginning of January he had been trying to capitalize the popularity of King William by proclaiming him Emperor of Germany or Emperor of the North German Confederation. There was some support for, and much opposition to, this course, which Clarendon, the British foreign secretary, deprecated as likely to cause a fresh crisis with France. Bismarck was still pushing the plan in March 1870, and the glorification of the dynasty was no doubt one reason why he was looking hopefully at this point on the idea of placing a Hohenzollern prince on the Spanish throne.

This was to supply the occasion of the Franco–Prussian war, and two points are beyond question : Bismarck undoubtedly instigated the candidature, and he undoubtedly welcomed the outbreak of war which resulted from it. The dramatic episode of the Ems telegram in July 1870 gave him extreme pleasure, and he loved to tell the story in later years, with increasing distortions. Some historians have recently shown a curious reluctance to accept the Spanish story at its face value, and have endeavoured to prove either that the whole affair was an example of brinkmanship which went wrong, or even that Bismarck's aims were peaceful and defensive, and that no one was more surprised than he at the result. This is a strange reading of the movements of the most calculating brain in Europe. Bismarck did not make that sort of mistake, although we can point to many examples in his career of tentative moves and soundings which failed to produce results, and of vindictive courses unnecessarily prolonged because of his own combativeness and irritability. What we seem to have in this case is another example of his skilful pursuit of alternative courses. There were two essential possibilities : either that France would acquiesce

in the Hohenzollern election, in which case Prussia would
be no worse off, and there would be gains in influence and
prestige; or France would not, in which case there might
be war, for which he was ready. What we must reject is
the assumption that he was innocently unaware of this
second possibility.

Following the Spanish revolution in September 1868
the Spanish leaders, Marshals Serrano and Prim, had
approached Prince Leopold of Hohenzollern-Sigmaring-
en, after unsuccessful soundings in Portuguese and
Italian quarters. He was the son of Prince Charles
Anthony, prime minister of Prussia during the new era;
the family was Catholic and Leopold was married to the
sister of the King of Portugal. Bismarck welcomed the
candidature from the start, insisted that it was purely a
matter for the Hohenzollern family, and soon had evidence through Benedetti of Napoleon's uneasiness at the
prospect. But the prince was unwilling, and although his
father hankered after acceptance the King of Prussia
confessed in March 1870 that he was 'utterly against the
affair'. On the 9th Bismarck produced some very respectable reasons for acceptance : improvement of Spanish–
German trade relations, strengthening of the dynastic
cause generally (for Spain might otherwise become a republic), diversion of French forces and attention from the
Rhine, thus strengthening the prospect of peace. Even
dear old King William could see the weakness of these
arguments, and he pointed out sharply in reply that if
Leopold lost the unstable Spanish throne as he well might
do, Hohenzollern prestige would not be helped : nor
could he guarantee Spanish aid against France. But the
King met Bismarck, Moltke, Roon, and others at dinner
on 15 March and found them unanimous for acceptance,
and he hedged to the extent of promising his consent if
Leopold accepted. As a result of the continued pressure
from Spain and Bismarck's persistent encouragement of
the Spanish government's aspirations, Leopold finally did
so; Bismarck assured Charles Anthony on 28 May that
Prussian interests would be served. Bismarck had sent

Lothar Bucher and a staff officer, Major Max von Versen, to Madrid, and the two agents were active in encouraging Prim and also Charles Anthony.

Bismarck's subsequent conduct is compatible with the view that he was alive to all the possibilities of the affair, and ready for whatever followed. He steadily denied (right to the end of his life), that the Prussian government had played any part in the candidature, and he lied like a statesman to this effect in the Bundesrat on 16 July. It was clearly necessary that Prussia's role should appear a passive one, while French offensiveness was stressed as much as possible. He arranged for the King to visit the Tsar at Ems at the end of May; this satisfied him that the entente with Russia was in working order, and he naturally did not say anything to suggest that he was seeking war with France. He then withdrew to Varzin, drinking bottles of Karlsbad water as a mode of convalescence after a bad attack of jaundice which had put him genuinely out of action in April. Unfortunately there was muddle in Madrid; the Cortes dispersed, owing to a misunderstanding, before Leopold's acceptance could be put to it; the secret was known in Paris on 2 July, and it fell to a new foreign minister, the Duke of Gramont, to direct the whirlwind that followed.

The public reaction in France was violent; undoubtedly there was a slightly morbid fear of encirclement by Hohenzollerns. This made it more difficult for the French government to move gingerly, but in any case Gramont, believing ardently in the Austrian alliance, determined to carry things through with a high hand, and he carried Napoleon and Ollivier with him in the process. His immediate protest to Berlin was published in the French government press, and Benedetti was then instructed to persuade King William to dissociate himself from the candidacy. On the 6th, Gramont said in a speech that France's interests and honour were imperilled. At Ems, William was not pleased with the French demands or with Gramont's speech, and days of crisis followed, while Paris raged and the French authorities prepared for war.

Charles Anthony, however, withdrew the candidacy on behalf of his son on the 12th, and Bismarck, worried lest the King's courteous bearing and desire for peace might look dangerously like surrender, bombarded him with advice to say as little as possible. He returned to Berlin on the 12th, and, fearing another Olmütz, even contemplated resignation. The situation so far had raised the prestige and morale of the French government; it now made the mistake of demanding positive assurances. Gramont asked the French ambassador for a letter of apology from William to Napoleon. Benedetti was instructed to go to the King and secure an assurance that he would not authorize a renewal of the candidature. William, accosted in the street on the morning of the 13th, refused Benedetti's request. Bismarck at the same time had begun to plan a diplomatic counter-attack which would emphasize Gramont's offensiveness and put the French in the wrong. Then later in the day came the telegram from the Foreign Office official, Abeken, giving the news of Benedetti's latest demand, and by judicious deletions and abbreviations Bismarck gave the King's action the appearance of a refusal of further negotiation (instead of a mere breaking off of that particular conversation). The amended telegram was published at once. Now France must draw back, or fight; she could not retreat, and declared war on the 19th. One of Bismarck's first acts was to publish the text of the French proposals for compensation which Benedetti had written down and handed over in August 1866. So began Bismarck's third war. It was certainly not an unprovoked attack on Prussia's part : but who can deny that Bismarck's conduct since 1866 had provoked the provocation?

The story of the Franco–Prussian war belongs to military history. In a sense it might be said that King William was the biggest problem that Bismarck had had to face in bringing the war about, as he had been in 1866. Bismarck kept near to the King at headquarters during the war, wearing his general's uniform and getting in the way of the army commanders, who as usual wanted no interference by civilians. The fighting in August made the French defeat a certainty; the swift Prussian progress kept Austria neutral. Bismarck's main political activity was to prepare for the setting-up of a German Empire; this led to some typical negotiations whereby the four southern states were safely gathered in. In contrast to his attitude in 1866 he showed less sensitivity to the feelings of the defeated power, and very much more towards the touchy and thin-skinned southerners, whose particularist feelings had not been drowned, although they had been submerged, in the wave of nationalist enthusiasm.

The vital fact was that the four states all rallied to the national cause in July 1870, and their troops fought as ardently as the Prussians, Saxons, or for that matter the Poles. Bismarck saw to it that the negotiations for their entry into the Reich were completed while the war was in progress. Baden and Hesse made no difficulties; but Bavaria had to be bribed and cajoled with substantial concessions, including a separate postal service and the freedom of her army from federal control in peacetime. The promise of heavy secret payments (which came from the *Welfen-Fonds*) helped to convert the impecunious King Louis II, and an agreement was signed on 23 November 1870. Thus isolated, the King of Württemberg hastened to adhere two days later. The King of Bavaria was even persuaded to write a letter in the name of the German princes, inviting King William to take the imperial crown. The King acquiesced somewhat ungraciously, for he hated the thought that Prussia would be absorbed in the new state. A Reichstag deputation begged him on 16 December to accept, thus recognizing that the crown was, in form at least, the gift of the princes. With deliberate offensiveness towards the beaten French, the new German Empire was proclaimed in the Hall of Mirrors at Versailles on 18 January 1871.

There was no interest on this occasion in a lenient peace. On the contrary, many arguments and calculations led Bismarck to the view that a well-dramatized triumph over France was politically necessary, and this released him from the need to impose any curb on his own vindictiveness. He remarks in his memoirs, 'I never doubted that the victory over France must precede the restoration of the German kingdom, and if we did not succeed in bringing it this time to a perfect conclusion, further wars without the preliminary security of our perfect unification were full in view'. After some tentative calls for annexations in the German press in July, a fierce and widespread demand for the cession of Alsace and Lorraine began after Sedan, and Bismarck encouraged it with inspired articles. Treitschke in a famous essay insisted that the German-speaking population of the two provinces merely showed by their loyalty to France that they did not know what was good for them. To keep this nationalistic fervour at its height it was necessary for Bismarck to play up the idea of an age-long struggle, and Ranke in due course won universal German approval with the dubious historical verdict that the 1870 war was fought against Louis XIV rather than Napoleon III. It followed that conditions of peace must be sufficiently rigorous to guard against a war of reassertion or revenge on France's part and also to show that Germany's leaders were themselves convinced of the existence of a deep-seated French hostility. The National-Liberal leaders joined in the demand for the two provinces.

The Second Empire collapsed on 4 September, and after the crowning French disaster of the surrender of Metz on 27 October there was no real hope of a recovery. But although talks began with representatives of the interim government in September, the German demand for the cession of Alsace and Lorraine prevented an early conclusion of peace. In order to calm the apprehensions of other governments Bismarck repeatedly assured them that in spite of the irredentist demands in the press, military considerations alone were involved in the decision as to the new Franco–German frontiers. The chauvinistic excitement was on balance more useful to him than embarrassing, for he was able to claim that he had given way to irresistible demands. The peace of Frankfurt, finally concluded on 10 May 1871 after a preliminary treaty in February, gave Germany Alsace and eastern Lorraine, with Metz and Strassburg, although France retained Belfort. This concession and a reduction of the indemnity balanced the retention of Metz, and finally secured Thiers' reluctant signature. Nevertheless, the indemnity was considered a crushing one at the time, and as we shall see was intended to give the German government a hold on the defeated French for many years to come. Until payment was completed, France would have to submit to an army of occupation.

No one could doubt the vast significance of the German victory and its diplomatic aftermath. In the House of Commons on 9 February 1871 Disraeli said that the balance of power had been entirely destroyed, and the country that had suffered most from the change was England. France, Austria–Hungary, and Russia could make the same claim, and with greater reason. The victories of 1866 and now of 1870 had transformed the political geography of Europe. A great new military power had been created, pressing against three international frontiers which had hitherto been free from serious danger of attack. To this had been added the revolution in military logistics which had indeed been anticipated by the use of railways in the Franco–Italian and American civil wars, but which had now been thoroughly advertised by Germany's central position and explosive efficiency. But these developments, looking outwards from Germany, meant that the new state in its turn was threatened from three directions. The Germans in their earlier, disunited condition had always felt insecure; now the mighty Reich gave greater protection, but also a more powerful circle of possible enemies, who would soon no doubt copy her military techniques. So with the creation of the Empire there was created the apprehension that was to haunt it continuously in the future : the fear of encirclement, the nightmare of coalitions.

The result in the case of both Germany and her neighbours was a greater overall sense of vulnerability, but also, and particularly in Germany, a greater sense of opportunity. There were dangers everywhere, but Bismarck had shown men how to triumph by boldness and cunning. Unfortunately for these adventurous spirits he had himself reached the point beyond which expansion seemed unprofitable and dangerous. France for her part had been thrown back, after fifty-five years of rather shaky recovery, to the humiliations of 1815, but with the difference that whereas her earlier failures had been due to an international coalition, now her embittered feelings were concentrated on one enemy alone. Bismarck was to spend the next twenty years in a state of baffled irascibility, as he sought to give his creation the security which continued to elude it in spite of his triumphs.

Chapter Four

The Chancellor and the Liberals

LORD ODO RUSSELL, a pleasant man, had talks with Bismarck at his headquarters at Versailles in December 1870. Bismarck knew well enough what the British Foreign Office wanted him to say, and it was not to his interest to upset them; so the Englishman was assured that the new empire would be peaceful. The Germans now, Bismarck said, would be solely employed in organizing their political strength at home and would resist any engagements to fight other nations abroad; and 'having no conquests to make for themselves will only care to resist invasion, while the conquest made by others will be indifferent to them'. This was one of many statements in which Bismarck insisted that the new empire would be a 'saturated' or satiated state, satisfied with her new boundaries, concerned only to enjoy a peaceful and prosperous future. Could it be true? Did Bismarck really know where and when to stop?

It seems that he did, against all probability as it appeared to many people at the time. History records the fact that after becoming Chancellor of the German Empire on 18 January 1871 he fought no more wars, and when he retired in 1890 there were nineteen years of peace to set against the provocative diplomacy and three wars of his first eight years of office. But it is also true that until at least the end of the eighteen-seventies he kept everyone on edge with his old virtuosity, and that he could not have fought a fourth war without bringing a coalition into existence against him. So as he was certainly not born peaceful we can ask whether he achieved peace or had peace thrust upon him. He was what he had always been, vindictive, dominating, a violent man and a splendid judge of political opportunities. The man had not changed. But clearly his fortunes had; and there were a number of obvious reasons why further wars should be avoided.

One was a sheer absence of worthwhile opponents. He had imposed his will successfully on Austria and France, and unless either of these chose to launch a war of revenge (he professed to believe in the early possibility of this as far as France was concerned), there was evidently nothing to be gained by fighting them again. There was no earthly reason for quarrelling with his other great neighbour, and in any case a war with Russia would bring France and perhaps Austria in to attack his rear. There were some great German nationalists who wanted to incorporate in the Empire the German Austrians or Balts or even the Dutch or the German Swiss; the demands for Alsace-Lorraine had given an opening for irredentist talk about other objectives. But it is quite certain that he had not the faintest desire for any such embarrassing additions at the risk of an armed coalition of the powers against the new empire. On the other hand there was a heavy programme of tasks at home in organizing the new state.

There were also reasons of a more personal nature for a judicious change of role at this stage. His successes, in spite of his apparent recklessness at times, had been due to great skill in isolating domestic as well as foreign opponents; he had retained the invaluable support of the King and the army, and had even won over the National Liberals. But he had at the same time been adding steadily to the list of enemies and disillusioned friends. Success had thus brought its own retribution; and in the diplomatic field, whether he quite realized the fact or not, his room for manoeuvre had now become very narrow indeed. He had reached the point at which almost any move on his part would automatically arouse the deepest suspicion; any offer of collaboration would suggest a trap; the fate of Benedetti and Beust and Rechberg and all the others who had gone for rides with this tiger would be remembered as dreadful warnings.

Things were not quite the same at home. His successes had created wild popularity, and he had many admirers. Secure in the regard of the Emperor, he was now at the summit of political authority and social standing. He received the Iron Cross, First Class, as a Christmas present from the King of Prussia in December 1870; he was created a Prince in March 1871, and presented with a large part of the domains in the duchy of Lauenburg in the summer. Here the estate of Friedrichsruh gave him a second large residence although he preferred Varzin, which he had so recently acquired. In spite of this eminence, he found plenty to worry about. There were many unsolved problems, some directly resulting from his own policy. Germany was still disunited : a national policy, with clear objectives and wide emotional backing, had been found hitherto only in foreign affairs, in resistance to real or imaginary threats. If he was to avoid international strife he must now find a convincing domestic programme to justify the new imperial government.

The popular enthusiasm for the army after its recent successes also had its dangers. He had succeeded in his three wars in maintaining the ultimate authority of the political leadership, but with increasing difficulty. The course of the French war had been punctuated by fierce disputes with von Moltke, who wished to keep to himself not only the direction and planning of military operations but also negotiations with the enemy which would undoubtedly involve major political results. Bismarck had finally forced the issue and secured the King's complete confirmation of his overriding authority in January 1871, so that it was Bismarck and not Moltke who negotiated the final armistice and peace terms. But in a fourth war the prestige of the generals and inclination of the King might relegate him to a subordinate position. Apart from his desire to preserve his own authority he was sure that the generals lacked political understanding. His alliance with von Roon as Prussian minister of war had been profitable, but as the minister was the spokesman of the army before parliament the General Staff regarded his office as a symbol of constitutional control, and strove persistently to reduce its importance. Bismarck seems to have watched this struggle somewhat warily, but he had no doubt that the position of complete independence of civil control in peace as in war desired by the General Staff was dangerous in itself, and threatening to his own position.

All this meant that he had to embark on a new policy and change his political methods. He had now to preserve and defend what had been achieved. Germany was a saturated state, the empire had been won, it needed peace and dependable allies. He had to show the same ingenuity in avoiding war that he had hitherto shown in bringing it about. He had to handle people in a different way, and win confidence; hitherto he had been seen in the opposite role, beating down opposition, sowing dissension, giving expression to his own natural inclination to violence. He had earned universal mistrust : now he wished to be believed. We cannot doubt that although he could understand intellectually the need for these more patient and conciliatory tactics, he found them extremely irksome, and he did not carry them out very convincingly at first.

In foreign affairs he may have recognized at once that he could no longer use war as an instrument of policy, but he certainly continued to use the threat of war for some time, and it was only after some humiliating rebuffs that he discovered the embarrassing consequences of unsupported menace. The position was complicated by the fact that in domestic politics he saw less need for restraint, and in some measure transferred to the home front the violence and shock tactics that he had mainly directed into diplomatic channels in the past. Altogether the change of course was dictated more by reason than by temperament and there can be no doubt that the next five or six years, when he was trying to gain his ends by these somewhat changed methods, were the least successful in his career. He seemed to have become unexpectedly clumsy, to have lost his touch and some of his tactical skill, and to be continually misreading the minds of his neighbours and opponents.

Partly no doubt this was due to an inevitable relaxation of the tight hold that he had hitherto kept on his temper, at any rate in dealings with his more influential and senior contemporaries. In the past he had shown deference not only to King William but also to such elder Prussian statesmen as the Gerlachs, and to eminent foreigners, including Gorchakov and Napoleon. Holstein overheard a conversation in 1863 in which Ernst Ludwig von Gerlach remarked kindly to Bismarck, 'You're a most promising young man, but . . .'. As he rightly remarks, Bismarck needed the self-control which he undoubtedly possessed at the outset of his political career in order to endure such a superior attitude. But he adds that after 1871 he never heard a single example of similar self-control on Bismarck's part. On the contrary, 'I gradually formed the opinion that he sought the reward for his achievements in refusing to bow to anyone's will but his own, and in obliging everyone with whom he had official contacts to comply with his whims'.

He started satisfactorily, however, by securing his constitutional position; the constitution of the new empire was virtually that of the North German Confederation, extended by treaties to include the four South German states, Bavaria, Baden, Hesse, and Württemberg. After submission to a newly elected Reichstag it became law on 20 April 1871. The Liberals had hoped to extend parliamentary control by judicious pressure when such revision took place, but they had to accept the essential features of the 1867 constitution. So Bismarck ruled, with the authority and backing of the Emperor; there were no ministers besides himself, and departments continued to be run by officials responsible to him, and not to the Reichstag. There was therefore no cabinet for the empire, and no chance of a development of political experience by the party leaders, as under the English system, or, in a different form, under the American. Bismarck was above party and above the parties, and although he had the support of majorities in the Reichstag he could, with the Emperor's backing, get on without them if necessary. The effective imperial body was the Bundesrat, or Federal Council, over which he as Chancellor presided. The Reichstag continued to be a talking shop, which the Chancellor and other officials could attend and address without taking part in the debates; its power of effective action hardly went beyond throwing out the budget.

The imperial government controlled foreign trade, policy, and diplomacy, the armed forces, war and peace, civil and criminal law, and taxation for imperial needs. But the position was complicated by the continued existence of the twenty-five states which made up the empire, each with its social system, often an old established dynasty, its own constitution, and the rights to legislate on and administer local affairs. The political systems of these states varied greatly. Prussia, in spite of its unreformed constitution, still based on the narrow three-class suffrage of 1850, was by no means the least democratic. The Prussian administration remained strongly conservative. The secretaries of state running the imperial departments were usually members of the Prussian government, in which Bismarck continued to hold the office of prime minister and foreign secretary. The Prussian government remained in effective charge of many imperial matters. Thus the Empire was truly an enlarged Prussia : and although the Prussian delegates had only 17 out of 58 seats in the Bundesrat, their numbers and influence were sufficient to allow them to veto amendments to the constitution, and generally to dominate its proceedings. The next largest state, Bavaria, had only six delegates.

If the German people were prepared to accept this system, which fell so far short of complete parliamentary democracy, it was because they felt the need to leave responsibility to their leaders for the time being. The theory of the *Rechtsstaat*, which sought to guarantee basic individual rights in a benevolent and beneficent state, clearly owed its vogue to the age-long tensions of

German political life. It seemed advisable to entrust power to reliable leaders in the face of danger, and there can be no doubt that the very brilliance of Prussia's successes since 1866, far from relieving apprehensions, had produced new anxieties, stimulated by the conviction (Germany did not differ from many other new states in this) that the world was envious. However, it was also satisfying that solid legislative work was going on throughout the seventies to provide the empire with a centralized legal system. This was primarily a matter of unifying relevant features of the widely differing systems of the individual states. The result was a series of common codes for the empire in commerce and industry, with a new uniform currency and a uniform system of criminal law. A Supreme Court was established at Leipzig. Bismarck was willing to allow the National Liberals to make themselves useful with this unspectacular and often highly technical work, under the general direction of Rudolf von Delbrück. So the *Rechtsstaat* took shape.

But it was unreformed Prussia, and the Prussian army, and the drive and ingenuity of a Prussian statesman, which had created the Reich, and this was the real source of the government's authority and strength. If it was a police state it was also, and more obviously in the eyes of its people, a state of warriors and efficient bureaucrats; and their patriotic deployment of leadership and power gave the people something to be proud of, and something to imitate. To the foreigner, and particularly the Frenchman, there came in time the feeling that there was something a little inhuman in this persistent cult of efficiency and military strength; but it was not until after the disasters of the first world war that the Germans themselves began to have second thoughts about their enthusiastic acceptance of the new imperial role. 'It was enough that military manners and bearing should permeate the people, so that even the civilian learnt to click his heels together and bow with the requisite stiffness' wrote Eugen Diesel disapprovingly in 1931. 'This persistent interference on the part of the Prussian State mechanism soon began to have an unfortunate effect on the life and manners of the people. The conversational tone became loud and brusque; arrogance and ostentation were to be met with everywhere.'

But in the eighteen-seventies the critics were few and far between, and were of interest to the disillusioned Germans of the post-Nazi era mainly because of their rarity. Apart from a few theologians and scholars such as Karl Christian Planck, who criticized the new Germany on ethical grounds, there was Friedrich Nietzsche, who thought that Bismarck's Germany represented the most stupid and mendacious form of the German spirit : 'I shall forgive no one who makes a compromise with it.' 'Listen to the barking commands that virtually encircle the German city, now that there is drilling outside every gate', he wrote a little later. Georg Gottfried Gervinus, an influential historian who had hoped for Prussian leadership of united Germany in 1848, deplored both the militaristic and anti-federal trend of Prussian policy after 1862, and in 1870, just before his death, submitted a memorandum to the King of Prussia warning him against the dangers of the centralized warrior-state which was likely to follow the victory over the French. Heinrich von Gagern, who had been President of the Frankfurt assembly in 1848, and the poet Georg Herwegh can also be noted as deeply disillusioned men. They were scarcely noticed, and the splendours and indeed divine sanction of the Bismarckian achievements were proclaimed by Treitschke and many other loud and powerful voices.

Germany could also look with satisfaction on her rising economic power. There had already been a steady and substantial growth of the economy between 1850 and 1870. When J. M. Keynes said in 1919 that the German empire had been built more truly on coal and iron than on blood and iron he apparently meant to argue that the economic victories after 1871 were of more enduring value than the victories of Bismarck and Moltke in diplomacy and war. These, however, had themselves been helped by the earlier phases of economic expansion in the fifties and sixties; Moltke's campaign plans for example took full advantage of the substantial railway building. The achievement of a united empire undoubtedly gave a fresh stimulus to development. But while the overall picture between 1870 and 1914 is one of remarkable growth the actual course of economic development during the greater part of Bismarck's chancellory, right down to 1890, was less satisfactory. After a short boom period there came a great economic crisis in 1873 followed by only a partial recovery : there were recurrent set-backs alternating with periods of slow advance and it was not until the mid-nineties that the really rapid and sustained phase of expansion began.

It is, therefore, easy to misread the overall figures. Statistically the facts are striking. The German population of just over 40 millions was still only a little more than that of France in 1871; by 1914 it had increased to nearly 68 million, while that of France had remained almost stationary. 64 per cent of the German population had been agrarian in 1871; 60 per cent was urban in 1914. The output of pig iron increased from 1,564,000 metric tons in 1871 to 14,794,000 in 1910; coal output from 29 million in 1871 to 191 million in 1913; railway lines from 18,000 kilometers in 1870 to 59,000 in 1910; gross registered mercantile marine tonnage from 9,000 in 1870 to 4,400,000 in 1913. This extraordinary growth placed her level with, and in some directions in advance of, Britain in an economic success story which is bettered only by that of the United States in the same period. Among other things it enabled her to develop a great armaments industry and to find the men for even larger armies, so that her military potential increased disproportionately to that of all her European neighbours. For Bismarck, however, this industrial development was a source of new political problems rather than a cause for jubilation, and the growing pains of the national economy in the first years of the empire had in fact soon to be added to his list of worries. He was glad at this period to leave economic policy as far as possible in the admirable hands of Rudolf von Delbrück, whose free trade principles satisfied the liberals. But in economics as in politics things took a depressing turn after 1873.

Bismarck is unlikely to have shared Treitschke's belief in 1870 that henceforth German policy could hardly commit any mistakes. In the state of nervous exhaustion and irritability which followed the war he soon had reason to worry about the behaviour of France. France was required by the peace treaty to pay an indemnity of five milliards of francs (£200,000,000), in fixed instalments at certain precise dates, neither before nor after, over a period of three years; no payments on account were permitted, nor could they be made in any medium except gold or silver, or German thalers or florins. A contemporary English estimate put the costs of the war to Germany, direct and indirect, at about £115,000,000. Germany therefore stood to make a handsome profit, and in fact the total amount finally paid by France, with interest charges and supplementary expenses, was about £212,645,000; so that Germany made something like £100,000,000 on the transaction. The undoubted purpose of this apparently onerous 'war-fine' was, however, to keep France thoroughly under German control, for the occupation of French territory by German troops was to continue until payment was complete. The sum, which seemed—and indeed was—a vast one for those days might be expected to cripple France for some years if her finances were as shaky as they had appeared to be in the last years of Napoleon III's reign. Irregularities in payment, which were obviously anticipated at the German headquarters, would make possible continued German interference in French affairs. In fact, France showed a positive enthusiasm for paying her debts, and Bismarck was soon facing the awful thought that this unnatural zest was proof of a deep rancour against Germany which might foreshadow early preparations for a war of revenge.

He was already rumbling angrily to his close associates at the end of 1871 as to the need for a preventive war, and as the French government's plans to rebuild its army on the German model became clearer during 1872 and 1873 the Prussian generals too began to talk ominously of a further war. Meanwhile the indemnity was rapidly ceasing to be an effective weapon. According to the more picturesque version the thrifty Frenchmen, digging deeply into their hoarded savings, rapidly subscribed the funds that their country needed. This is true only to a limited degree. The French government raised three great loans to pay off the three instalments, the first being borrowed from the Bank of France in June 1871 and the other two coming from public subscription in 1872 and 1873. The second loan, issued on 28 July 1872, was oversubscribed twelve times. Various devices, including liberal commissions to induce foreign subscribers to take part, helped to secure this success; French prestige could not afford a failure. The purchase in London of bills on Germany was greatly helped by German indebtedness to England as a result of the short loans which the Prussian government had raised in England to finance the war. It is true that France merely exchanged creditors, but she preferred to be in debt to the international money market rather than to the German government.

It is now evident that Bismarck and the Prussian experts, more accustomed to great-power politics than to great-power economics, had quite failed to understand the ramifications of the international credit system. They had failed to ruin French commerce and credit; indeed, the indemnity transactions, by absorbing surplus French credit, saved France from the consequences of the world-wide slump which hit Germany particularly severely after the boom of 1872.

Bismarck was thus forced to accept the last of the French payments in the minimum time; but the completion of the evacuation of German troops from France on 15 September 1873 did not bring any improvement in Franco–German relations. He continued to hurl threats and warnings at the French government, vetoed plans for intervention in Tunis in 1874, and finally destroyed any hope of an early reconciliation. It is just possible that a milder bearing might have achieved this; at any rate, he started, six years too late, to woo the French after 1877. Whether the French would ever have forgiven him is doubtful, but the chance that he could persuade them that his quarrel had been only with the discredited Napoleonic regime was thrown away by the peace terms and his subsequent conduct. At the same time he could not bring himself to crush France in a second war. German diplomacy henceforth had to revolve round the assumption of a permanent French enmity which might very well lead to the war of revenge as soon as allies could be found. To prevent this, Bismarck must turn his diplomatic talents to the gathering of all potential allies into a combination friendly to his country.

The essential basis of this combination seemed to have been found in the formation of the so-called three emperors' league (*Dreikaiserbund, Dreikaiserbündnis*) in 1873. The friendly understanding with Russia of 1868 had served Bismarck's ends well enough in the recent war; and if the Russian government had not in fact been called on to restrain the circumspect Austrians it had done nothing to give encouragement to the French. Russia had her *quid pro quo* in German support at the London conference of March 1871 which freed her from the Black Sea clauses of the treaty of 1856. Franz Joseph recognized that the game was up and that there would be no revenge for Sadowa; when the efforts of Count Hohenwart to establish political understanding with the Czechs fell through he completed his alliance with the Magyars by dropping Beust as Chancellor (he was sent as ambassador to London) and entrusting the foreign ministry to the gipsylike but unadventurous Magyar aristocrat, Count Julius Andrássy, in November 1871. The Magyars had no quarrel with Germany. Their bugbear was Russia and the Panslav cause; and while expediency dictated a working alliance with the Habsburgs they had no desire to oblige the Emperor by fighting Sadowa over again. They were more kindly disposed towards the Turks than to any of their European neighbours, and Andrássy's greatest problem came when the Emperor desired in 1878 to annex a Turkish province full of unwanted southern slavs. Andrássy's first diplomatic move is significant : he sounded Granville in December 1871 as to the possibility of an Anglo–Austrian understanding, and although he had no success he tried again on other occasions.

Franz Joseph and Alexander II both invited themselves to the autumn manoeuvres in Germany in 1872, and during a conference in Berlin in September the first sketch of an agreement was examined, based on the well-tried but incontestably vague principles of the Holy Alliance of 1815. A Russo–German military agreement was signed at St. Petersburg in May 1873, and the Tsar then visited Vienna, where he proposed a similar military pact to Franz Joseph without telling him of the recent agreement with Germany. When this was declined an alternative, purely political, plan was devised, and this was acceded to by the German Emperor on 22 October 1873 after being signed by the other two. The most striking fact about this agreement is that it agrees about nothing in particular; each of the three wished for some hold on the others, without being able to say so, and they had nothing to unite them against the rest of the world. There were expressions of concern at the spread of revolutionary socialism, although in fact the movement was in decline after the expulsion of Bakunin and his followers from the First International at the Hague congress of 1872 and the subsequent removal of the International to New York, followed by its dissolution in 1876. The terms of the Austro–Russian agreement provided for the concerting of action by the two powers even when their interests differed; and mutual consultation, followed if needed by a special convention for military co-operation, in the event of aggression by a third power. Now, which would such a third power be? Turkey perhaps; but she was hardly an aggressive power these days. But what of Germany?

Undoubtedly the agreement had the character of a

defensive or precautionary measure on the part of Austria and Russia; neither could be free from apprehension as to what Bismarck would do next. If they wished to place themselves on friendly terms with him they also thought it desirable to draw together so that they would not be left to deal with him alone in any future crises. It suited Bismarck to join such a grouping; he could interpret it as a guarantee against French aggression, for it could at least be assumed that the willingness of the others to join was automatically proof that they would not join France. If they fell out, however, both would seek his support, and, if he failed to give it, would probably seek that of France. On the other hand he was soon to realize that it was equally not to his advantage that they should become too friendly, and be able to dictate to him or ignore him. A Turkish crisis would probably divide them sufficiently to make them dependent on his mediation, but it might also face him with intolerable pressure to take sides. He had to steer a dangerous course among these diplomatic rocks; and it was not altogether reassuring that the two powers were to show during the next three years an unwonted concern to work together in damping down any fresh crises in the Near East.

But there were even more dangerous rocks and whirlpools to circumnavigate at home. For while he could be satisfied with merely avoiding crises abroad he felt himself faced with a challenge to the empire by the Papal leadership and the new, pro-Catholic, Centre party. This he decided could not be shirked. The struggle, which started as a domestic German campaign against 'ultramontanism' (looking beyond the Alps to Rome for guidance), soon became linked with France, and culminated in a series of painful rebuffs for him in 1875.

To understand this we must first look for a moment at the unstable balance of political forces in the new empire. Bismarck had the support of the National Liberal party, which was the strongest in Germany, with 120 seats in the Reichstag in the election of March 1871; but this was in many ways an unnatural partnership for a man of his outlook and purpose. He had himself undermined their position, first by denying them the full expression of their political ideals in the 1867 and 1871 constitutions, and then by giving a lead to more democratic political forces with the introduction of universal suffrage. They had many representatives among the rapidly growing big business and industrial elements, and were therefore the enemy of the socialists. Karl Marx and his followers after 1848 had been active in the south, while Lassalle's more moderate and pro-unionist movement had made headway in the Protestant north, leading to the formation of his Workingman's Association in 1863. After his death in 1864 his followers found a leader for some time in J. B. von Schweitzer, an even more convinced supporter of Bismarck's programme than Lassalle. A Marxist party was launched in 1869. The two socialist parties continued in rivalry for some years, exchanging dialectical insults, but they began to win seats in the Reichstag, two in 1871, nine in 1874. They amalgamated in 1875, and finally called themselves the Social Democratic party in 1890. Bismarck feared this development as much as the National Liberals, who, he did not fail to note, were also being threatened from the Centre and the Right.

The Conservative party, which had not changed very noticeably from the standards of the Gerlach brothers, Stahl, and the *Kreuzzeitung*, was sadly disappointed in the Chancellor, who did not now seem to share their single-minded devotion to Junkerdom, the Prussian state, and the agricultural interest; they were doubtful about the moral basis of his *Realpolitik*, and in spite of their Protestantism disliked some aspects of his quarrel with the Catholic church. They were alarmist in foreign policy. They disliked his concessions to the Liberals. But his separation from them was always a little surprising, and it would not be difficult to repair. The *Reichspartei* was a section of the Conservatives which did support him, and offered a convenient bridge. The austere group of the liberals which had not compromised in 1866 or later, the

Fortschrittspartei or Progressives, showed on the other hand no inclination to make themselves useful to anyone. Finally the new Centre party was vigorous and expansive, and carried out throughout the early seventies a spirited offensive against Bismarck himself and his National Liberal supporters.

This party was the expression of the strong and varied political interests of the Catholics in Germany, and would have played a vital role in the new empire whatever Bismarck's relations with the Pope. There was a widespread movement throughout Europe for the organization of political Catholic interests against the challenge of the modern world, and the German party in this sense shared in a broader development. But it had a strong local mandate. After the Reformation Protestants and Catholics in the Holy Roman Empire had preserved a rough balance of forces and this had continued in the Confederation after 1815. The line of the Main in 1866 left the North German Confederation predominantly Protestant; the accession of the four south-western states to the new empire in 1871 while Austria was excluded left the Catholics in a minority, although a large one. The Catholic Centre party was formed in December 1870, with a programme which placed in the foreground of the rights of the church, but also challenged the secular, centralized Bismarckian state by affirming opposition to civil marriage and a preference for decentralized administration, a federal state, the harmonizing of the interests of capital, landowners, and workers, and the protection of working-class interests. Shortly after this they merged with the small group of irreconcilable Hanoverian opponents of Prussia, the Guelphs led by Ludwig Windthorst. They also had no hesitation in working with other small opposition groups, such as the Poles. Bismarck could hardly have failed to treat the party as hostile to himself, but his inclination to do so publicly was very much increased by the recent turn in Papal policy.

The assertion of the conservative or ultramontane position had started in 1864 with the encyclical *Quanta Cura* and the issue of the famous Syllabus of Errors, and Pius IX had, after long preparation, brought his campaign against the liberal tendencies inside the Catholic church to a triumphant conclusion with the Vatican conference, which convened on 8 December 1869. The Syllabus had denied among other things that the Church could come under civil government. The Council produced a long and acrimonious controversy over the dogma of papal infallibility among the 764 great ecclesiastics who attended, but formal approval was finally given on 18 July 1870, at the very beginning of the Franco–Prussian war. Only a small number of German Catholics—who formed the 'Old Catholic Church'—refused to submit.

There was undoubtedly much apprehension in Europe at the time—and not only in Protestant Germany—as to the interference in secular politics that might follow the acceptance of the dogma, although in fact this was to prove quite unfounded. But it might bring strength and comfort to the Centre party, and a further objection to the papal initiative was that it might well encourage the French. Bismarck could not ignore this Catholic problem, but with his usual instinct for keeping alternative lines of policy open he first tried to bargain with the papal authorities. He had made repeated attempts in the past to persuade the Pope to influence the Catholics in the Prussian parliament in his favour, and he promised the Pope asylum in Germany in November 1870 after Italy's absorption of the papal states had raised the possibility of his withdrawal from Rome. He let the Archbishop of Posen know however that he looked for the support of the 'ultramontane clerical party'. Nothing came of this, and from the summer of 1871 onward Bismarck showed his hostility to the Centre party openly.

The party was already formidable, having secured fifty seats in the Prussian diet, and 63 seats in the new Reichstag, in March 1871. It constituted the obvious opposition to the strong central government, based on Liberal support and the army, which he was creating; and he needed a domestic enemy to rally popular opinion now that the succession of foreign opponents had served their turn. So a struggle was probably unavoidable, but there were more ways than one of conducting it. Bismarck chose to launch a campaign of destruction against the party and the Catholic interests, and in this instinctive choice of a stand-up fight he was responsive to his temperament, for he was applying in domestic politics the tactics of uncompromising struggle that he had applied to his foreign opponents hitherto. Having chosen to live peacefully with his neighbours abroad he was declaring war on his rivals at home. But the issue was a confusing one to many people, and by no means entirely domestic; it soon became linked in Bismarck's mind with the French, and if he took really seriously the belief in an international Catholic conspiracy against the new Germany it was not even a domestic issue primarily. Many people abroad, critics in other matters, approved his conduct; they included Gladstone in England. There seemed no doubt that he had not misjudged the popularity of the campaign. Odo Russell, who had just come to Berlin as the British ambassador, wrote in March 1872 that the joy and enthusiasm at Bismarck's declaration of war on the Church were even greater than that which had preceded the wars with Austria and France. And he noted 'the almost juvenile ardour with which the "new man" is discussed at Berlin'.

The Catholic Church had a privileged position under the Prussian constitution with extensive rights which were fully exercised. On 8 July 1871 the special division for Catholic affairs in the appropriate Prussian ministry was abolished, following an attack in the *Kreuzzeitung*, and support was given to the Old Catholics. Bismarck openly attacked the Centre party in the Prussian chamber in January 1872 and this was followed by the expulsion of the Jesuit order and the breaking off of diplomatic relations between Germany and the Papacy. The appointment of Dr. Adalbert Falk, a member of the Ministry of Justice and of the *Reichspartei*, as Prussian minister of religious affairs, was followed on 8 February 1872 by a short school-inspection bill which launched a legislative campaign against Catholic privileges. Falk, an earnest and hard-hitting politician, a year later introduced an elaborate series of measures which became law in May 1873, and were followed by others in May 1874 and May 1875. In the meantime Professor Rudolf Virchow, an eminent pathologist but also an active Progressivist deputy, had described the campaign as a cultural battle, a *Kulturkampf*, between the forces of obscurantism and enlightenment. The four May Laws of 1873 opened the real attack. They required the formal submission of the church authorities to the state, and when this requirement was generally resisted, heavy penalties followed.

But Bismarck had other problems, apart from his health, which necessitated frequent periods of rest at Varzin. The struggle against particularism was not confined to the Catholic church; he had to seek means to neutralize the Prussian Upper House and its aristocratic supporters if his national reform plans were to develop. This seems to have been the explanation of a crisis in the autumn of 1872 over the Administrative Districts bill which was defeated by a combination of Catholic and Conservative votes. Its purpose was to reduce the autocratic powers of the Junkers by introducing a measure of representation into Prussian local affairs, and it had the support of the Liberals in the Lower House. The fact that Bismarck was away from Berlin when the voting took place puzzled many people, and there were rumours of a 'serious illness'; the British ambassador was taken aback when Bismarck returned a few days later apparently in the best of spirits. The explanation seemed to be that he had staged the parliamentary crisis to force the hand of the Emperor, who would not otherwise have been ready to quarrel with the faithful Junkers; indignant at their opposition to his government, he now agreed to create sufficient new peers to ensure the passing of the bill. Bismarck decided now to hand over the office of prime minister of Prussia to von Roon; this was primarily a tactical move to avoid the continuous triangular bickering between himself, the Emperor, and the exasperating Prussian ministers, but he hoped that it would spare his temper and his time. He remained foreign minister of Prussia. This was a miscalculation on his part; Roon was loyal in his fashion, but his sympathies were conservative, he had with difficulty accepted the School-Inspection bill, and the effort to use him as a means of manipulating the conservatives increased Bismarck's irritability, rather than otherwise. Roon retired into private life at the end of 1873, and Bismarck, who had spent most of the preceding ten months at Varzin, resumed the office of Prussian prime minister, and held it until his retirement in 1890. But the tension with the Junker conservatives was not eased, and they were angry when he proceeded to hound out of office an admittedly indiscreet man, Count Harry Arnim, German ambassador to Paris from 1871 to 1874.

They also looked with some suspicion on his handling of the army. Bismarck had grumbled that the Centre party wished to create a state within the state, but this was even more true of the military hierarchy. Their feeling against him had not diminished after the French campaign, and General von Stosch, Chief of the Admiralty from 1872–1883, was being discussed as a likely successor. The military cabinet, headed now by General E. L. von Albedyll, continued to find the war minister's responsibility to parliament irksome, but their main preoccupation was to ensure the virtual passing of the iron budget in perpetuity, thus securing the automatic grant of 225 thalers per man for an army equivalent in size to 1 per cent of the population. This it will be remembered had been granted for four years in 1867, and the law had been extended in 1871 for another three years. In the autumn of 1874 an attempt to get a bill accepted fixing the size of the army until the government saw fit to propose a legal modification was fiercely attacked by Eugen Richter, spokesman for the Progressives, and he was supported by the Centre party and the left wing of the National Liberals, led by Eduard Lasker. There seemed to be looming up a renewal of the fiery constitutional struggle of 1862. The Emperor warned the generals to be ready for a fight. Bismarck, again conveniently ill, had left them and their spokesman in the Reichstag to struggle for a time with the opposition. On balance it is evident that he disliked the complete irresponsibility of the generals even more than he disliked parliamentary control. At last, when the affair had reached something of the status of a major crisis, he intervened, proposing as a compromise that the government's bill should be voted for seven years. At the same time he rounded on Lasker, whose followers, he said, had been elected under his banner and on the strength of his reputation. The bill went through, supported now by the united strength of the National Liberals. They felt they had triumphed. Bismarck on the other hand could tell the Emperor that the principle of the bill had been secured. It was his victory, on balance; some check on the soldiers had been preserved.

And in the meantime the *Kulturkampf* was at its height. In May 1873 Marshal MacMahon's election as President of France, with the support of the clericals and monarchists, appeared to foreshadow a monarchist restoration. It would probably have taken place if the Comte de Chambord could have abandoned his sublimely ridiculous insistence on his own flag. MacMahon's election and the imminent ending of the German occupation had encouraged the French clerical press to sympathize openly with the German Catholics; and the French bishops also began to issue pastoral letters condemning the anti-Catholic legislation. When the Bishop of Nancy called for public prayers against the loss of Alsace-Lorraine to Germany, Bismarck demanded sharply that the French government should restrain its bishops. But he accepted the explanations of the French foreign minister, the Duc de Decazes, fairly readily in January 1874, for he had no desire to drive France further into the monarchical camp. MacMahon was now regarded as the sole bulwark against a monarchist restoration, which again seemed the prelude to a war of revenge. In the Reichstag elections in January

1874 the Centre party increased its seats from 63 to 91. Nevertheless, all this failed to convince Bismarck that it would be expedient to ease the tension inside Germany. On the contrary, Falk was left to harry the Catholics with redoubled vigour.

The finings, imprisoning, and expulsions of bishops and priests accordingly went on. A series of actions against Cardinal Ledochowski, the defiant Archbishop of Posen, who was threatening those who accepted the new laws with the greater excommunication, entered their last stage at the beginning of 1874. Sympathizers at first paid some of his fines, but they had increased to over £4,000, and could only partly be covered by the sale of his goods. He was then confined to a fortress. Archbishop Melchers of Cologne was equally defiant. He and the bishops of Paderborn and Trier were also imprisoned. There were riots in Westphalia when the Bishop of Münster's furniture was sold. The Prussian authorities went steadily on until by the end of 1876 the whole organization of the Prussian Catholic church seemed to be shattered; and yet the church was as strong as ever—the Centre party even stronger. Fines of millions of marks were imposed, although much of this was not collected because of the flight of the accused. One thousand and three hundred parishes were deprived of their priests. Monasteries had been dissolved; all the bishops except four had gone—to Heaven or to exile.

It is impossible to reduce this story to one of clever political manoeuvring on Bismarck's part. Historians have been so accustomed to talk of his political genius and sense of realities that even his failures are assumed to be based on some bold and subtle plan. Some have argued that his real aim was to isolate France and that the attack on the church was intended to draw Italy, Austria, and Russia to his side. Certainly the Italian government's relations with the Pope were strained, and the Tsardom in its Greek Orthodoxy did not look with any pleasure on the activities of the Vatican, nor on ultramontane Catholic influences among the Poles. Where Austria comes into this picture is not clear, but the argument presumably is that if Italy and Russia sided with Germany, Austria would have to do the same. There is no doubt that Bismarck welcomed the formation of the three emperors' league as a means of ensuring the continued isolation of France, and he had convinced himself by the beginning of 1874 that the ultramontanes in France, as well as the monarchists, were a threat to peace. By forcing the French government to restrain the ultramontanes he had driven a wedge between them, and this can be considered a use of the *Kulturkampf* to further a diplomatic end. It is also argued that he left it to Falk to conduct the campaign in Prussia, and did not approve of some of his steps. But these views leave out of account the fact that the campaign was launched before he had begun to worry seriously about France's recovery, and that his repeated talk about Germany's future role as a satiated state shows his desire after the victories in France to represent himself as a peacemaker, while the furious battle with the Vatican was bound to contradict any such view. Moreover the admirers of Bismarck cannot have it both ways: it is impossible to praise his mastery of Germany and at the same time say that it was all Falk's fault. His violent reactions certainly do not suggest that he was merely allowing events to take their course.

The explanation that seems to fit the facts best is that he launched the campaign primarily for reasons of domestic politics; it promised to put him at the head of a popular, national Protestant crusade against the combined enemies, as he saw them, of the Reich, and it failed largely because his nerves and passionate irritability led him to exaggerate and misjudge the issues, and to create fresh sources of opposition. It would seem that he quite failed to understand the character and resources of the Pope, who proved himself a terribly annoying opponent, a combination, as one writer has said, of obstinate meekness and flaming indiscretion. The two continued to complicate the struggle and get on each other's nerves with all the varied resources of their peculiar diplomatic genius. The attempt on his life by a young Catholic working man, Kullmann, in July 1874 seems finally to have convinced Bismarck that Germany was indeed the victim of a great Catholic conspiracy, and that he alone could save his country. His nerves almost gave way under the strain. The public was equally excited, seeing Jesuit conspiracies everywhere; Odo Russell noted in the spring of 1874 that a popular lion which had died in the Zoological Gardens was believed to have been poisoned by Catholics. The repressive measures increased. In the meantime he brooded over France's rapid recovery and military reforms, and discovered new sources of ultramontane conspiracy in Belgium.

Things were evidently moving towards some sort of crisis, which Bismarck hoped would take the form of a Catholic collapse. Instead, he was himself diplomatically outmanoeuvred by the French, and suffered what he regarded as a public humiliation in the early summer of 1875. This was the affair, still rather mysterious in spite of much study of the documents by historians, of the so-called 'War-in-Sight' crisis. He had reached the state of believing the most extraordinary reports and rumours, and he was now conducting high politics with little of his old tactical deftness, but rather with a rough heavy-handedness which probably shows over-confidence in the strength of his position. His extraordinarily long absences from Berlin prove indeed that there was no threat to his tenure of office at home, but they may have left him imperfectly informed as to swiftly changing moods abroad. Yet he knew enough to be uneasy about the general position at the beginning of 1875. There was a certain lack of warmth in Russo–German relations, and Bismarck sent von Radowitz, one of the abler German diplomats, to St. Petersburg in February to rekindle it; the mission, if that was its purpose, was not a failure, but it did not secure for Bismarck a free hand against France, as some believe was its purpose. Bismarck was convinced that the French were working energetically to secure Russian backing, and he was right in so far as the French ambassador in St. Petersburg did receive from time to time kind and friendly but non-committal words of encouragement from Gorchakov and the Tsar.

At any rate, Bismarck was showing increasingly open hostility towards France from the beginning of the year, and this culminated in a war scare in April and early May. On 11 January the French national assembly began to discuss a bill to reorganize the army, and this was passed; there was great excitement at the end of February at the news that German horse dealers had received orders to purchase 10,000 army mounts for the French army, and Bismarck forbade the exportation of all horses from Germany. Then too the French government was said to be hoarding a vast sum in 20 franc notes, it was thought as pay for the troops. Another story, which Bismarck produced later, was that the London *Times* had been bribed by a large sum to print correspondents' letters dictated by Decazes, who wished to cause a scare in order to further his speculations on the Bourse. Bismarck's alarm at French conduct was certainly strengthened by the grimly pessimistic reports of von Moltke, and there were the usual assumptions as to ultramontane machinations to push France into war. Belgium's behaviour also alarmed him and he demanded that the Belgian government should restrain its bishops. It was claimed in Berlin that all the dissatisfied German Jesuits and priests were making Belgium their place of refuge, conspiring there with the French clergy against the German empire, and encouraging the annexationist party in France to revive the plan which Benedetti had submitted to Bismarck in 1866. The Belgian government kept its head, and replied that there were not more than twenty German Jesuits in the whole of Belgium, including the students.

The affair became an international crisis when the Berlin newspaper, the *Post*, published on 8 April an article entitled, 'Is War in Sight?' and concluded that it was; France was preparing for a war of revenge. The article was written by a Prussian official and publicist,

Konstantin Rösslev, on Bucher's instructions. The *Kölnische Zeitung* followed, in the same vein. This produced tremendous excitement : was the German government preparing a case for a preventive war against France? At a dinner on 21 April the experienced diplomat Radowitz, who should have known better, said to the French ambassador that if France had any ulterior motives of revenge at all (obviously she had) it was Germany's duty to crush her before she could carry out her design. No foreign government believed for a moment that France was preparing war, but their ambassadors in Berlin had to listen to a surprising flow of free and rather agitated talk about French intentions from Moltke and Bismarck and others. It was in these circumstances that Decazes appealed to the British and Russian governments for support, thus greatly complicating the issue and leading to the interesting theory that the whole crisis was due, not to German aggressiveness, but to a clever French move to score a diplomatic triumph at Bismarck's expense.

It is argued in support of this view that the excitement created by the *Post* article died down rather quickly, certainly by the middle of April, and that Radowitz was merely stating, in a private conversation and in response to a question, what he claimed to be the views of the majority leaders in the Reichstag. And Decazes certainly told Gontaut-Biron in a private letter of 29 April that he meant to use the Radowitz episode to 'crystallize' the attitude of the Russian cabinet. He admitted that 'the immediate danger has disappeared'. On 6 May the *Times* printed an anonymous article, written by its regular correspondent, H. G. de Blowitz, on Decazes' prompting, alleging that the war party in Germany was planning a new invasion. But even if Decazes was rather less worried at the moment than he professed to be he may still have had genuine fears as to what Germany was planning, and from the more long term view of French interests it was obviously wise to secure a demonstration of support abroad if he could. And Bismarck, who had so often out-manoeuvred the French, should not have been so furiously angry when the French, for once, outmanoeuvred him.

It has been suggested that much of Bismarck's agitation and fears were due to the extreme inaccuracy of his secret agents, who undoubtedly brought him some wild stories (such as that of the Belgian plots). Some of the rather indiscreet talk in Berlin may have been due to a lack of co-ordination between the politicians and the soldiers. Bismarck seemed to have been obsessed primarily with the Catholic issue, Moltke with French military power, and although the two sources of apprehension co-incided in suspicion of France, he may have failed to prevent some carelessness by the soldiers; Moltke made no secret of his belief in the need for a preventive war. The Emperor insisted the war was unthinkable. The Crown Prince agreed. We are left with the conclusion that if Bismarck was really planning war he had gone about it very clumsily, and if he was not he had laid himself open to a rebuff; in short, he had misjudged the situation.

Gorchakov, who had accompanied the Tsar on a visit to Berlin, carried out the Tsar's instructions to secure assurances from the German government, and Odo Russell too was instructed to offer the British government's help in removing misunderstandings. Bismarck's famous interview with Gorchakov on 8 May certainly produced the necessary assurances, but Bismarck was said to be beside himself with rage, while the Russian chancellor, a malicious, bright-eyed little man, bantered him and told him not to lose his temper! Later Bismarck spread the story that Gorchakov had sent off a telegram beginning with the famous words, 'now peace is assured'; if he had done so this would certainly have been a very conceited action on his part. But this seems to be the Ems telegram technique over again : Bismarck was abbreviating a quite innocuous statement that the Russian Emperor had left Berlin perfectly convinced as to the conciliatory dispositions which reigned there and which ensured the maintenance of peace. This was the end of the crisis, and

Bismarck withdrew to Varzin for six months to walk off his exasperation.

The war-in-sight crisis is on the face of it so trivial that its significance can easily be lost. It did not end the *Kulturkampf*; the struggle inside Germany continued until Bismarck began to show signs of second thoughts on the issue after 1876. Nor did it ease his mind in any way about the French : at the beginning of 1877 he was so alarmed at the prospect of a French attack that he sounded the British government as to an offensive and defensive alliance to meet this contingency. It was the republican victory at the polls later that year which reassured him, for he had always believed that the monarchists were the warmakers in the new France.

And yet the events of 1875 are of great importance. The French had secured a demonstration of goodwill greatly strengthening their confidence and sense of security; Russia, Britain, and even Italy had given warnings, plain enough in spite of much polite language, that they could not contemplate anything like an unprovoked German attack on France. Hitherto Bismarck had succeeded in isolating his opponents, or perhaps had been clever in taking advantage of their knack of isolating themselves; but now his reputation had caught up with him, and they were even anticipating moves which he perhaps did not intend to make. He had become the victim of his own reputation. He chose to believe that he had been the victim of Gorchakov's malice, and this is a second major consequence of the crisis; from this point his distrust of Gorchakov, which existed already, begins to influence Russo–German relations until it led to a major breach between the two countries. And a third consequence was a new regard for Austria, for she, alone among the great powers, had refrained from intervention, saying that the German assurances already received were sufficient.

But all this was in depressing contrast to the exuberance and self-confidence of 1871, and we may pause here to speculate as to Bismarck's reputation among historians if he had retired from politics at this stage. There had been frequent offers on his part to do so; one obscure resignation crisis in March 1875 lasted a week, and he again asked to be released in May, on grounds of failing health. The Emperor wouldn't hear of it, and Bismarck was to enjoy, groaning under his burdens, many more years of office, and to make many more offers to retire. Yet the verdict, if he had gone at this point, would surely have been unfavourable; it would have been that he could create an empire, but could not run it successfully. The economic depression, the French revival of confidence and power which he could not check, the increasingly violent, embarrassing, and futile struggle with the Catholics, the discreet hints of foreign disapproval which he could not castigate or defy, and to many people the beginning of fresh trouble in the advancing power of the Socialists, were all pointing to the conclusion that the business of running an empire was beyond him. The Clericals certainly thought so, and were telling themselves that Lucifer had fallen, never to rise again.

It was the feeling also among diplomatists that he had lost control of the situation and of himself. 'Behind our backs Bismarck raves like a maniac', wrote Odo Russell to Robert Morier in May. Andrássy remarked that Bismarck, although 'always unscrupulous and cynical, had until lately acted with coolness and judgment, whereas within the last six months his good sense seemed to have entirely deserted him'. Peter Shuvalov, the Russian ambassador in London, rather an admirer of Bismarck, thought him a little out of his mind at times. Gorchakov, not an admirer, thought that he was suffering from over-drinking, over-eating, and lack of sleep, and needed a thorough rest. His health has to be taken into account; biliousness, toothache, nervous irritability, and insomnia were the price paid for thirteen years of success and worry. However, he did not retire; and as always in his great career, his mind was in control. No doubt there was more than one way to run the affairs of a satiated state. He spent six months in relative seclusion at Varzin (with many visitors) from 5 June until 21 November 1875. He seemed as gloomy as ever on his return : but soon there were signs of a re-shaping of German policy.

Chapter Five

Bismarck at his Zenith

THE three problems which he had to face were the maintenance of a successful tenure of power at home, the balancing of antagonisms abroad, and the state of the economy. The first was the problem of dealing with the Centre and Socialist parties, the second the problem of Russia and France, the third the problem of the state finances and agriculture. Between 1876 and 1879 there is a gradual change of course in each of these fields, with a movement towards the Catholics, Austria, and protection; but the moves were not hurried, and it is not clear how far they were concerted. Altogether they amounted to a major change of course. His actions seem to be rather less governed by passion and rancour than they had been in the early months of 1875, although he indulged himself plentifully in private tirades against the Empress Augusta and Gorchakov, and some of his other favourite aversions.

The resignation of Rudolf von Delbrück in April 1876 may or may not have been due to ill-health; Bismarck had not asked for it, but on the other hand Delbrück, who had so long been his closest collaborator, did not consult him about it. The usual view is that, being essentially a civil servant, Delbrück had decided to retire when he sensed a desire on Bismarck's part to get rid of him or of the policies that he represented. But nothing very definite emerges in domestic politics until 1878, and in the meantime Bismarck continued his extraordinarily long absences from Berlin, while keeping a watch on the foreign situation, which seemed to be drifting towards a general war over the Near East.

The long absences were not exactly holidays. During

the seventies he still spent most of these retirements at Varzin, which had the advantage of being much less accessible than Friedrichsruh, his new estate in the Sachsenwald in Lauenburg. The village of Varzin, a few houses with five farmers and some labourers, woke up to a considerable bustle of activity when he was in residence. Policemen, unneeded otherwise, put up at the village inn to protect him. The village post office was kept hard at work; for instance, during his stay of five or six months in 1877, it had to handle some 6,500 letters and 10,000 telegrams. Work, he complained, followed him like a shadow.

Bismarck's normal day at this period started with an English breakfast between 10 and 11 a.m. at which he ate lightly, and took the opportunity to read his letters; afterwards he dealt in his study with the business of his estate, talking to officials and workpeople, and later in the morning worked on any official papers that needed attention. Between one and two he would walk or ride in the neighbourhood. Luncheon was at 2 o'clock with his family, and guests, if any; afterwards he again retired to his study, or took another excursion, alone or with a guest. Dinner, at which conversation might be lively, was served at 7 o'clock, followed by coffee in the next room; while the guests talked (frequently in whispers), Bismarck retired to a small sofa and smoked one of his three long porcelain-headed pipes, usually taking little part in the general conversation. After about an hour he retired, and did not join the Princess for tea, which was served at 10 p.m., although he might drink a glass of milk. Everyone was in bed before midnight. He was now over sixty, rather unhealthily fat it would seem, continually tormented by neuralgia, bad legs, and stomach troubles, much of it caused, he insisted, by his pitiless master, who continually over-worked him.

It is always said that Bismarck managed the Emperor skilfully; he once told Ludwig Bamberger that he was much more of a courtier than a statesman. The Emperor however did his own share of managing. He maintained

his distance and his authority. He had his own maddening
ideas about foreign policy. He played the game of con-
sidering Bismarck's resignation offers gravely, and firmly
and invariably rejecting them.

During 1876 and 1877 he was more than usually exasperating on a number of occasions, thus necessitating
more frequent visits by his nerve-racked Chancellor to the
firs and green fields and beech trees of his estate. Bismarck took the cure at Gastein in the summer of 1877
with good results; he slept much better afterwards for
one thing. But it was the malice or obtuseness of his rivals
and critics and even sometimes his friends that upset him.
He was not losing his combative spirit, but he was increasingly conscious of the need to defend what he had
created rather than to expand further.

The danger to his creation for some years after 1875
seemed more likely to arise from a collapse of European
peace and of the system of diplomatic understandings
which he favoured than from direct attack. The basis of
this system was the vague agreement between the three
empires to work together, and in June 1875 a revolt
against the Turkish authorities in Hercegovina, which
quickly spread to the adjoining province of Bosnia, raised
the problem of how to cope with an eventual collapse of
Turkey, which seemed increasingly probable during the
next twelve months. Russia and Austria might quarrel
over the spoils and this might force Germany to take sides
or to stand by while some unacceptable changes were
made in the map of Europe. Other possibilities included
French intervention on one side of the other, or perhaps
Italian support of Russia against Austria. But these were
his more permanent underlying apprehensions, and were
rather remote ones at the moment; his immediate cause
of uneasiness was that, far from quarrelling, Russia and
Austria were agreeing rather too easily with each other.

Bismarck contributed to this *rapprochement* by his long
absence from Berlin in 1875; he was inaccessible, and his
deputies in Berlin were painstakingly reticent. The Austrian and Russian governments both showed genuine

anxiety to damp down the Balkan crisis, and it was the stubborn refusal of the Bosnian insurgents to go home, and what appeared to be the approaching collapse of the central Turkish government through bankruptcy and an- archy, that forced them to confer and make plans. The first result of this was the so-called Andrássy note to the powers of 30 December 1875, setting out a rather sketchy plan of reform which it was hoped would be acceptable to all parties in Turkey, without embarrassing the great powers too much. It was the result of amicable discussion between Andrássy and Gorchakov, and Bismarck readily agreed, promising to support anything acceptable to his two allies. But although he continually protested Ger- many's complete lack of interest in the Balkans, he was very much concerned that Germany should not be left in the cold.

Accordingly he turned to England. But what exactly he wanted has never been clear, and it led the British prime minister, Benjamin Disraeli, to chase the will-o'- the-wisp of an Anglo-German alliance fruitlessly for the next twelve months. Bismarck had warmly approved Dis- raeli's purchase of the Suez Canal shares in November 1875, and on 2 January 1876 he told Odo Russell (a good example of his deceptive frankness) that 'Germany could not well afford to let Austria and Russia become too intimate behind her back—nor could she let them quarrel with safety to herself'. He would be prepared to resist 'the annexing tendencies of Austria and Russia in Turkey' if he were sure of British support. But according to a Russian account he spoke rather differently to d'Oubril, the Russian ambassador, some two days later. After com- menting on the curious fact that Andrássy, usually so indolent, should have shown this sudden energy in pro- posing Turkish reform, he suggested that Andrássy's posi- tion would be eased if Austria–Hungary could round off her territory in Bosnia, while Russia took compensatory advantages in Bessarabia. Germany would not object, and he was sure that England would not worry about such trifles, if she could safeguard her interests in Suez. He asked only to be left to talk the Englishmen round.

There is an obvious contradiction between his promise to England to join her in preventing the partition of Turkey, and his offer to Russia to support it. But his talk to Odo Russell had also broached in the most delicate possible way the need to be prepared for every contingency, which might mean that his real aim was to lead the British government by easy stages towards a partition policy. But why should he bother? The clue may simply be that Gorchakov and Andrássy had been getting on a little too well in December, and he knew, remembering the tensions of 1867, that an agreed policy of partition, although it would avoid a major crisis between his two neighbours, could hardly fail to lead to friction, and a corresponding strengthening of his position as a mediator. It would be useful too to have Britain in tow. All these possibilities were obvious to Gorchakov, who promptly rejected Bismarck's suggestion. Disraeli continued to believe that an agreement with Bismarck was just round the corner, while Bismarck continued to speak of his desire to follow England's lead but also of his difficulty at any given moment in securing the Emperor's agreement to anything objectionable to Russia.

Probably then this small burst of activity on his part at the beginning of 1876 was due to nothing more than his desire not to be left out of the picture, and it is not typical. As the Near Eastern situation became increasingly tense his views and support were sought by both his allies and by England, but it is impossible to point to any positive help that he gave to any one of them. He had no bias in favour of Turkish independence, and he found partition a useful topic of conversation on occasion; if in the course of time it really took place he would perhaps gain advantages as a mediator, and there was something to be said for the idea of diverting his neighbours' attention away from central Europe. In the eighties he was to seek to divert French and British energies and mutual animosities into north Africa for the same reason. On the other hand there were two dangers to be avoided at all costs : one was the descent of the powers into a general war over Turkey, the other the aggrandisement of Russia at Austria's expense. This led to some anxiety behind the scenes to give Austria good advice but it did not produce any overt hostility to Russia, although the Russian diplomatists were grumbling from October 1876 onward that his professions of goodwill were never followed by deeds.

The crisis took a turn for the worse in the summer of 1876. The Bosnian insurgents would still not lay down their arms. A further reform plan, again sponsored by Andrássy, was supported by Gorchakov and Bismarck, but because in desperation it contained the vaguest hint of a possible coercion of the Turks it was rejected by Great Britain in May; Disraeli, on no very sound evidence, was convinced that this was a shock to Gorchakov and a delight to Bismarck. After the end of June news of Bulgarian massacres committed by the Turkish troops in the previous April and May horrified Russian and British opinion. Sultan Abdülmecid was deposed, as was also his successor in August. Serbia and Montenegro declared war. Disraeli, far from being the fanatical anti-Russian and pro-Turk that his critics believed, was trying secretly during June to reach an agreement with Russia for the setting up of some form of self-government for Bosnia under Turkish suzerainty. But the Austrian and Russian Emperors preferred a more far-reaching bargain between themselves, and this took the form of the Reichstadt agreement of 8 July 1876, with a plan for the rearrangement of Balkan territory in the event of a Turkish collapse, which now seemed imminent. This was substantially what Bismarck had proposed in January, but he played so little part in all this that he was not even told of the agreement until mid-September, when Andrássy let the cat out of the bag, without Gorchakov's consent. It is nevertheless a tribute to Bismarck's fame that no one in Europe doubted his dominant role behind the scenes in all that was going on.

The more the crisis is studied, however, the more evident it becomes that he carried caution to the point of abdicating any real attempt to influence events. The problem that faces the historian is to decide whether, as the Russians came increasingly to believe, this reserve was not in itself an act of hostility towards them. A curious incident on 10 July 1876 might be said to illustrate both attitudes. Bismarck persuaded Odo Russell to go with him from Kissingen to Würzburg to persuade the Emperor not to send a diplomatic note to the British government criticizing its conduct. During the three-hour train journey Bismarck fumed with rage and nervousness, and said repeatedly that he would have to resign; he valued British friendship too highly to consent to anything that did not strengthen the ties with England. Odo Russell defended British policy to the Emperor, who dropped his plan; on the return journey Bismarck was again calm and pleasant. Ostensibly this was a pro-British gesture; it was to the same extent anti-Russian; but its purpose was probably to prevent a commitment to either side. Bismarck rejected the idea of an international conference in August, because he foresaw an embarrassing contest between Disraeli (now Lord Beaconsfield) and Gorchakov, in which he did not want to become involved. Late in September, when the Emperor's exasperating habit of family gossiping with the Tsar had led to an unwelcome enquiry as to whether Germany would support Russia in pressure on Austria, he was again angry with the interference and evasive in his reply. So was he also in October when Austria sought his support against Russia, and a further British attempt in November to tie him down to the understanding that he professed to seek was equally unsuccessful. In a speech in December 1876 he stated his position publicly, in a famous but often misquoted phrase: 'the whole of the Balkans is not worth the healthy bones of a single Pomeranian musketeer'.

There is nothing in all this to suggest that he had any aim other than that of keeping Germany and himself out of trouble. His vague promises of support to all the parties concerned were bound to lead to some disillusionment when they looked to him for more specific help; but it was about all he could do. He was again showing alarm at France's conduct and war preparations during the next few weeks and at the end of January 1877 offered Germany's benevolent neutrality to Britain if Britain were still seeking to restrain Russia. In return he asked for Britain's benevolent neutrality if France, relying on her *rapprochement* with Russia, should attack Germany. As Disraeli was still hoping to settle the crisis peacefully by persuading Russia and Turkey to accept a programme of concessions to the Christians in the Balkans he concluded that Bismarck's real aim was to push Russia into a war with Turkey in order to give himself a free hand against France. The German offer was not only rejected but was reported to the Russians. By now the Russian government, owing to strained finances and other troubles, had lost its zest for war, and if the Turks, who were in quite a fanatical mood, had accepted the very mild proposals put to them by the powers in March 1877 there might have been an end to the crisis. Bismarck's mediation, with judicious pressure on the Turks, could have been decisive, and would probably have earned him some genuine Russian gratitude. But he did nothing. On the other hand when Russia did go to war with the Turks in April 1877 he did not attack the French, as some people had anticipated. Instead he disappeared again on another long rest cure at Friedrichsruh and Varzin, from 15 April 1877 to 14 February 1878.

Thus it seems that we must abandon the myth, which historians are strangely reluctant to discard, of Bismarck's domination of events during the eastern crisis. His cautious, negative diplomacy is in striking contrast with his conduct of home affairs, which culminated in a public quarrel with General von Stosch, more threats of resignation, and many signs that some powerful new domestic storm was brewing. He was continually uneasy over the international situation, but could do little except watch and wait. At home he could take the initiative.

The Stosch affair was important mainly as a reminder of his dependence on the Emperor's goodwill, but the extent to which he pushed this particular 'Chancellor's crisis' suggests an attempt to consolidate his position in readiness for policy changes. Stosch was one of his colleagues, head of the Admiralty, a favourite of the old Emperor, and also intimate with the liberal circles surrounding the Crown Prince and Princess. Bismarck professed to believe that plans were on foot to install a 'Gladstone cabinet', his way of describing a government representative of a parliamentary majority, although he chose to interpret the term as meaning one dependent on Liberal and Catholic support. The link between the two elements was supplied in his view by the Empress Augusta and her immediate entourage, which included the Treasurer of the Household, von Schleinitz, and spread pro-Catholic influences into the very palace of the old Emperor.

So the early months of 1877 saw a good deal of agitated counter-measures by Bismarck, including the placing of articles attacking the Empress in the press through the agency of Dr. Moritz Busch; some of these are reproduced in Busch's memoirs. Stosch had in the previous year abandoned rather readily, on the request of Eugen Richter, the leader of the Progressives, certain budgetary provisions which he had previously wrung from the Chancellor. On 10 March 1877 Bismarck in a speech in the Reichstag openly attacked Stosch for this, remarking sarcastically that he had never anticipated that his own authority or persuasive powers would have less weight than Richter's with the naval administration. Stosch offered to resign; on 24 March the Emperor refused to accept the resignation; Bismarck then let it be known in the press that he too wished to retire. But the Emperor would not give way, and it even seemed for a few days that he would let Bismarck go rather than the favoured general. In the end it was agreed that Bismarck should take 'indefinite leave' and this explains his long absence from Berlin after 15 April.

Certainly it was the problem of the imperial finances which was uppermost in his mind at the moment; he was also critical of the Prussian finance minister, Otto Camphausen, who was showing signs of independent thinking on this question. Under the constitution of 1871 the cost of running the empire was to be met by indirect taxation on such things as beer and tobacco, supplemented by contributions (*Matrikular-Beiträge*) from the individual states. The advantage of this arrangement from Bismarck's point of view was that it prevented the Reichstag, elected by universal franchise, from using the direct control of taxation as a political weapon; the disadvantage was the necessity of asking for continued favours from the states and also having to ask for the Reichstag's agreement to the requests for the *Matrikular-Beiträge*. The revenues of the empire could best be strengthened either by a substantial increase in the indirect taxation or by protective duties, both of which, after being voted, could continue to be collected without annual grants from the Reichstag. The Liberals were uneasy at the prospect of a further reduction of parliamentary control and the Progressives thought indirect taxes inequitable in principle. But the case for protection had been strengthened by the depression since 1873, and in 1876 Windthorst, the astute leader of the Centrists, had opposed the abolition of one of the remaining duties, that on pig-iron. Thus a measure of protection would automatically increase his dependence on the Conservatives and his difficulties with the Liberals, but might facilitate agreement with the Centre. This would be useful, for the time had come, if not for a surrender to ultramontane intransigence, at least for skilful-obstinate negotiations over the Catholic issues which would involve compromise but consolidate some of the gains. A third problem that worried him was the advance of the Socialists, whom he had hitherto failed to coerce. A bill enabling the government to prosecute Socialist agitators had been rejected by the Reichstag in 1876, as a result of the opposition of Lasker and the National

Liberals. He had ample time to brood over these problems during his ten-months retreat.

The results began to show themselves in the New Year, and at intervals during 1878 and 1879. If we resist the tendency of Bismarck's admirers to cast all his actions into the heroic mould we must recognize that these decisions, although sufficient to amount to a major change of general policy, were sometimes of doubtful wisdom and frequently governed by quite unnecessary apprehensions. It is no doubt true, as Professor Werner Conze has recently remarked, that he had a high sense of his responsibility, which was deeply rooted in his Lutheran faith. He felt himself to be a statesman in the service of a righteous state, who stood above any and every party, and his domestic as well as his foreign policy after 1871 can be traced back to one single guiding principle, that of making the empire secure. The question is whether the dangers to it existed outside his imagination. How far were the *Reichsfeinde*, the enemies of the empire whom he so continually denounced, anything more than opponents of his own ascendency or policies? We do not have to assume that the dangers he discovered so frequently necessarily existed. His constant wariness was partly due to his memory of the earlier weaknesses of Prussia; now in the growing mood of exuberant self-confidence following the French war this continuing sense of danger on his part was beginning to appear out-moded and unnecessary.

Feeling his way with no fundamental policy beyond the security of the empire and his own position he may have gone further than he intended, and it is a great mistake to assume that he willed or foresaw the ultimate results of many of his policies. His immediate objective during the winter of 1877–8 seems to have been the strengthening of his own position in readiness for the changes in policy that he was contemplating; true to his well-tried tactics of examining alternative courses he sounded the Liberals while keeping the possibility of a conservative turn open. After two interviews in July and December 1877 he offered Rudolf von Bennigsen, the leader of the National Liberals, the post of minister of the interior. He also spoke of the possibility of making Bennigsen his deputy both in Prussia and the Empire. Bennigsen preferred the ministry of finance, and to this Bismarck seems to have demurred, but it would have had obvious advantages in binding his followers to accept Bismarck's financial proposals, or alternatively of providing means of expelling the more obstreperous ones from the party.

But the scheme went awry. On the one hand there was a letter from the Emperor reproaching Bismarck in such scorching and ungracious terms for his negotiations that he promptly had a nervous breakdown and a fortnight's illness, with the inevitable offer of resignation and a grudging half-apology from the Emperor. On the other, Bennigsen was not prepared to take office unless two of his most respected and experienced friends, Max von Forckenbeck and Franz von Stauffenberg, did so too. The Emperor was personally hostile to Bennigsen, and Bismarck had no intention of accepting any Liberal besides Bennigsen in his government; the plan had really died by the end of 1877, but he did not tell Bennigsen so for some weeks. On 22 February 1878, during a debate on a finance bill proposing increased duties on various articles including tobacco, Bismarck caused a sensation by repudiating his own colleague Camphausen, the Prussian minister of finance; he announced without previous warning that he wanted not only increased duties but a government monopoly of the whole tobacco industry. Camphausen resigned, and the National Liberals refused to accept the monopoly or pursue further the discussions about joining the ministry. Bismarck afterwards claimed that the Emperor would never have tolerated a Liberal ministry, but what is certain is that he himself had finally rejected the possibility of an English-type government.

After this signs of new political orientations began to multiply. The aged Pope, Pius IX, had died on 7 February 1878; his successor, Cardinal Pecci, who became Pope Leo XIII, wrote at once to the German Emperor proposing an improvement in relations. Studied urbanity on both sides soon replaced the former harshness, although progress towards a compromise settlement was slow and circumspect. It did not lead at once to political cooperation with the Centre party, which Bismarck desired; nevertheless, he could now extend his challenge to the National Liberals, who were unwilling to swallow either protection or the repression of the Socialists.

He had returned to Friedrichsruh and was again sourly contemplating the prospects when on 11 May 1878 a young exhibitionist, a tinker named Hödel, fired two shots at the aged Emperor in the Unter den Linden. No one was hurt. Hödel's political affiliations were varied and contradictory; his mental balance was questionable, and it was quite possible that he was merely seeking a brief enjoyable publicity. He represented no organized conspiracy. But Bismarck at once gave orders that a new bill restricting the activity of the Socialists should be introduced. The National Liberals were troubled, but once more rejected the proposal. Then on 2 June there was a second and more serious attack in the Unter den Linden on the Emperor by Dr. Karl Nobiling; the old man was gravely wounded, the assassin, who was apparently another crazy exhibitionist, committed suicide, and Bismarck decided at once to dissolve the Reichstag. His secretary, Dr. Tiedemann, tells us somewhat unkindly that it was only as an afterthought that Bismarck, after hearing the news, asked about the Emperor's condition. The election took place on 30 July, after a campaign in which Bismarck's influence, where it could be exerted through the press and his Conservative friends, was undoubtedly thrown against his former Liberal allies.

These somewhat macabre events provided a strange setting for the Congress of Berlin, a splendid international showpiece, the last of the series which had begun with the Congress of Vienna of 1814–15. Bismarck was the inevitable chairman, presiding over Europe while carefully advertising the crisis at home by displaying two loaded revolvers on his desk, and by other devices. He had come up from the country with a beard, and he startled the British prime minister, Lord Beaconsfield, by his vast size; he was no longer the slim man with a wasplike waist that the Englishman had last seen in 1862. As director of the negotiations Bismarck was arrogant, frank, and partly unsuccessful. Russia after winning the war against the Turks had overreached herself in the peace settlement that she imposed in March 1878, and the Congress had assembled to arrange, primarily on England's insistence, a scaling down of the demands made on the Sultan. Bismarck saw no advantage to himself or anyone else in a European war, and he favoured any bargains, reasonable or otherwise, which would provide a general settlement. He hoped that this would be the end of the eastern crisis. He hoped also to revive the three emperors' league, to bring Austria and Russia together again, and to secure for Russia sufficient gain to enhance the reputation of Peter Shuvalov, a man of charm and courage who at first seemed likely to be the leading Russian plenipotentiary and Gorchakov's successor.

Unfortunately Gorchakov himself decided to attend the congress, and Andrássy preferred to stand by the British. The substantial advantages which Shuvalov's quick wits and Bismarck's bustling chairmanship secured for Russia were not sufficient to prevent the blame for inevitable surrenders from being ingeniously diverted onto Shuvalov's shoulders by Gorchakov. Russia it is true regained southern Bessarabia, with Kars and Batum in Asia Minor; but Austria, without firing a shot, was allowed to occupy Bosnia, the British occupied Cyprus, and although a small Bulgarian state was set up south of the Danube, Turkey remained the ruling power in the Balkans. Although Russian opinion did not at first blame Bismarck for this partial defeat, disappointment was bitterly expressed by the Panslavists, and the Russian government gave vent to its outraged feelings by extremely obstructive tactics in the commissions which were sent to the Balkan peninsula to work out the new boundaries. Bismarck until the end of the year 1878 was still, however, hoping for a revival of the three emperors' league. He even encouraged the Tsar to send Shuvalov to Vienna on two occasions in order to talk Andrássy round to this. It was not until the beginning of 1879 that the continued isolation of Russia forced him to think more seriously of Germany's own position.

Domestic politics seem to have been his real preoccupation during the second half of 1878; even the Congress was a rather unwelcome distraction, as he did not fail to tell the other delegates. He hurried off to Kissingen as soon as the Congress ended on 13 July and although talks there with the papal representative, Cardinal Marsella, made no headway, the results of the election of 30 July were not unpleasing. The two Conservative parties gained 600,000 votes, with 115 seats in place of their previous 78; the National Liberals lost 30 seats and the Progressives 10, although together they still numbered about 140. The Social Democrats lost 3 seats out of 12, but practically no votes; the Centre stood firm. It was not very clear what he could make of the situation, or what he really wanted. His talks to Marsella show his desire to secure the co-operation of the Centre after a settlement in the *Kulturkampf*, but he was striving to undermine the faithful Liberals before a bargain with the Catholics had been secured. There was nothing he could do at the moment except to continue to work with them, and as they had been compelled to agree to legislation against the Socialists in order to hold their seats the anti-Socialist law could now be safely reintroduced. This 'Exceptional' Law 'against the dangerous activities of the Social Democrats' was passed on 18 October 1878. It provided for severe restrictions on Socialist activities, and was rigorously enforced by the police during succeeding years. It did not destroy the party; like the Centrists in the *Kulturkampf* it increased in number and in party discipline, and carried the bulk of the working class with it into permanent hostility to the Empire. But he also promised social legislation which would remove the revolutionary tendencies of the masses. It seemed that another corner had been turned; the Liberals had been confused, weakened, and brought to heel, the Socialists repressed, and in the process the way had been largely cleared for a decisive vote on protection.

So the last and most dramatic phase of Bismarck's change of course began. The necessary technical studies and legislation were not completed until the following summer, and with it there took place a major change in party alignments. Well-organized pressure by the manufacturers in favour of protection had been increasingly exerted since 1876, and we have seen that Bismarck's immediate concern for increased imperial revenue predisposed him in favour of this solution. By temperament he was hardly a natural free-trader or even a liberal, and as he grew older the increasing preoccupation with the jealous defence of the empire pointed to the strengthening of barriers around the national economy as well as around the vulnerable frontiers. He had found it useful to leave economic policy in the hands of Delbrück, the convinced free trader, before 1876, but he now conveniently underwent a process of conversion and self-education in economic matters, inspired largely by the leader of the Free Conservatives, Wilhelm von Kardorff, whose own industrial interests were extensive. Kardorff had founded the 'Central Alliance of German Industrialists for the Promotion and Preservation of National Labour' in 1876.

The agricultural interests, although slower to realize the possibilities of protection, were also becoming plaintive. Exports of corn were declining, and the farmers faced an increasingly hard fight after the middle seventies against the more cheaply produced imports from America and Russia. Nearly a million tons of Russian grain was imported in 1875, and nearly two million in 1877. The decisive event for Bismarck was the declaration of 204 deputies representing both agricultural and industrial interest on 17 October 1878 in favour of protection; the group which called itself the 'National Economic Union', included 87 Centrists, 75 Conservatives from both parties, and 27 National Liberals. The 204 made up a clear majority of the Reichstag, and on 15 December Bismarck was able to avow publicly his conversion to protection and to announce the programme that he proposed to follow. The aim was a moderate general tariff, primarily for revenue purposes rather than the defence of individual industries when they faced competition. He now worked on the detailed plans himself with great energy, and was ready to present the new legislation to the Reichstag in the following May, 1879.

At no stage in Bismarck's career is the problem of defining his ultimate aims and innermost thoughts more difficult; during 1879 he certainly introduced major changes in both foreign and domestic politics with every appearance of strong conviction, and yet in each case there are ample signs that the decisions may have been no more than passing expedients. Throughout he seems to be driven along by gusts of irritability against domestic and foreign collaborators, and it would be possible to see this as the real explanation of his decisions, were it not that he was also showing remarkable ease in forgetting past grievances (as in the case of Windthorst) when he chose. Some of these innovations, and in particular the choice of protection and the alliance with Austria, were to become in after years such basic elements in German economy and diplomacy as to make the original decisions appear much more inevitable and momentous than in fact they were. His tendency, in keeping with the *laissez faire* attitude of his generation, was to deal with each tactical situation as it arose (without thinking too much of the future except in conformity with the vague general aim of national security). One thing that he was certainly not planning in 1879 was the long-term development of German economy.

As his immediate purpose was to secure an adequate imperial revenue he preferred moderate customs duties on a wide range of commodities to high duties on a few luxury imports. This would spread the burden more evenly and lightly, but it would not seriously check imports in the interest of domestic manufactures. Thus although the iron duties were reintroduced the rate was fixed at the low figure of the late 1860s, in spite of the heavy propaganda of the leaders of the industry. The agriculturalists fared much better, and secured, with Bismarck's help, the greater profit from the political alliance of corn and iron on which the ultimate triumph of the movement depended. The corn duty saved the Junkers; it was the great landowners who benefited most, and the danger of their being economically squeezed into selling out to ambitious farmers and even peasants was largely averted. Bismarck may well have felt a more genuine sympathy for them than for the manufacturers. They secured in the last stages of the negotiations considerably higher duties than had been originally proposed.

The new tariff passed into law in July 1879. In the course of the debates, which he followed closely, Bismarck repudiated free trade as an example of the 'honourable capacity of dreaming' of the German race, threw over those Liberals who disliked the new policy, consolidated his position with the Conservatives, and secured the co-operation of Windthorst and the Centrists, although at a price. The ample revenues flowing in from the customs duties would have freed the government from all financial control by the Reichstag. Windthorst was able to check this process by an agreement that the surplus above a certain amount should be transferred to the treasuries of the states, and the machinery of the *Matrikular-Beiträge* would then have to operate if the imperial government wished for its return. This was little more than a book-keeping matter. The essential point was that Bismarck had preferred to make this bargain with the leader of the Centrists and not with Bennigsen, the leader of the Liberals.

There was thus a clear purpose and some elaborate political manoeuvring for practical ends in the protection issue, even if Bismarck's emotional journey to his goal appears puzzling at times. The great change in foreign policy in this year is harder to understand. His personal irritability resulted once again from the challenge of collaborators temporarily turned opponents; as in the case of the Austrians, the French, the opposition during the constitutional struggle, the Catholics, and more recently the Liberals he reacted fiercely and even vindictively to a challenge to his leadership. It was now the turn of the Russians to overplay their hand. They too like the Liberals were trying to dominate the relationship. Although after the crisis he was ready to renew the friendship they found, as the Liberals had done, that he had in the meantime reinsured himself elsewhere. But as in the protection crisis he was pursuing a number of advantages simultaneously. It is difficult to say which was the most important.

There is no doubt that the explanation which best fits the facts is that he had no long term aims at this point, but was drawn into a major crisis through his feud with Gorchakov and the Rumanian government. As in his struggle with the Catholics he soon began to exaggerate the ramifications of the reaction which he had himself created; and while the exaggeration was in part an expression of his own alarm it was also a skilful means of justifying his policy in the eyes of the Emperor or of doubting colleagues. He discerned behind Gorchakov a more sinister foeman in Miliutin, the minister of war, whom he regarded, quite wrongly, as the leader of militant panslavist elements. The crisis developed almost casually. Since the Congress he had sought as unobtrusively as possible to discredit Gorchakov, thus preventing his return to office after the long spell of leave that he was taking. But this was meant to pave the way for closer Russo–German co-operation. Gorchakov did return to office in December 1878, and Shuvalov's chances faded; Bismarck's undoubted goodwill towards Shuvalov had not been sufficiently tangible to give him any real diplomatic success. In a number of issues which arose in the New Year the German attitude seemed gratuitously provocative to the irritable and suspicious Russian authorities. Bismarck did not stage these crises to annoy the Russians, but he certainly used them to remind the Russians of his displeasure.

At the beginning of January 1879, when the special committee of the Bundesrat began its detailed elaboration of the tariff bill, the Russians at once took alarm. The tariff would hit Russia's valuable grain exports, and in the public debates Bismarck seemed to go out of his way to dwell on those aspects which would most irritate her. The Russian press accused him of wanting to start a tariff war, and although he showed at first an inclination to treat Russia's main export, rye, more leniently than wheat, he raised his demands later. A bill to unify railway freight rates, which was intended to prevent any evasion of the tariff by rebates, was also received by the Russians with outraged gloom. Then in mid-January there were reports that the plague had broken out near Astrakhan. After a hurried conference of Austrian and German experts in Vienna, strict measures to embargo certain Russian goods as possible germ carriers, disinfect other imports from Russia and scrutinize ships and suspected persons, were hastily drawn up and enforced early in February. Russian securities were hit, and again it was believed in Russia that Germany had acted with a deliberate lack of consideration; the Tsar said as much himself through d'Oubril. On top of this there came a third shock. On 4 February the text of an Austro–German treaty dated 11 October 1878 was published. It repealed Article V of the treaty of Prague of 1866, which had provided for an eventual rectification of the north Schleswig border. The treaty had in fact been signed on 13 April 1878, but Andrássy wanted it to be dated after the Congress in order to prevent charges of Austro–German connivance. Bismarck on the other hand wanted it dated before the announcement of the Duke of Cumberland's engagement to Princess Thyra of Denmark. The Duke was now the pretender to the throne of Hanover, and the engagement had revived Danish hopes. The Russian court had shown its sympathy for the duke, again to Bismarck's annoyance, although Queen Victoria had shown more active concern.

In each of these cases Bismarck could claim to be acting in Germany's interests; but he showed himself coldly indifferent rather than conciliatory towards Russia's not unjustified cries of indignation. Soon the fact that Germany was obviously not exerting herself on Russia's behalf over Balkan questions added to the indignation of the Emperor and the Russian press, and in April there were reports of Russian approaches to Italy for an alliance against Austria. The fact that these soundings, and some obscure conversations by the Russian General Obruchev in Paris in August, were apparently coming from the ministry of war confirmed his suspicions of Miliutin, which were increased when Russian forces on the Polish frontier were strengthened. The nightmare that now agitated him, in a situation largely of his own creation, was of war launched by expansionist, anti-German, revolutionary-minded Russian generals, ineffectually controlled by the senile Gorchakov and the enfeebled Tsar.

His quarrel with the Rumanian government was ostensibly over its failure to implement convincingly the provision of the Berlin treaty relating to the treatment of Jews. The real purpose was to secure better terms for German–Jewish business interests who had sunk capital in the Rumanian railways. It is an example of his new interest in economic policy. This might have formed a basis for co-operation with Russia, who had her own claims to press in Bucarest; and he had some difficulty in persuading Britain, France, and Austria, who favoured early recognition of Rumanian independence, to hold their hand. In order to keep up the pressure on Russia, a closer *rapprochement* with Austria, and some relaxation of pressure on Rumania, now seemed necessary, and the result was the Austro–German treaty of alliance of October 1879.

This famous alliance, which was to endure until 1918 and to form the solid foundation of an elaborate defensive system, grew in importance with the years, but we have to ask whether it was anything more than a temporary expedient at the time. Bismarck's planned offensiveness seemed to have succeeded when the Russian government made a conciliatory approach to him through the diplomatist Peter Saburov in September. He at once abandoned the idea of drawing Great Britain in as a third partner in an anti-Russian alliance and on 29 September even spoke favourably to the Austrians of bringing Russia into the Austro–German alliance as a third member. This Andrássy refused to consider, and the dual alliance was duly signed on 7 October; but Bismarck now concentrated, with the support of Saburov as the new Russian ambassador in Berlin, on the revival of the three emperors' alliance, which he finally achieved on 18 July 1881. On the other hand the dual alliance continued its separate existence, in spite of obvious Russian suspicions; thus we must assume that even if its immediate purpose in 1879 had been to bring Russia to terms he saw advantages in it for Germany which outweighed the danger of estranging Russia. And yet there seems no sign of a desire for a separate Austro–German alliance on his part before the quarrel with Gorchakov developed early in 1879. We must assume that the more general advantages of the alliance were of incidental interest at first, but rapidly became more evident. For it was soon seen to provide a working compromise between *kleindeutsch* and *grossdeutsch* sentiments, it eased the problem of reconciliation with the Catholics, and it freed him permanently of worry at the prospect of an Austrian *rapprochement* with either Russia or France.

Germany's position was very strong, and for that reason he could pursue alternative objectives and make awkward neighbours feel the weight of his irascibility. But he failed to get his way with the Russians. Although the aged Gorchakov was at last replaced by a conciliatory foreign minister in Nikolai Karlovich Giers the new Emperor, Alexander III, and his advisers viewed the alliance of 1881 as no more than a means of reinsuring themselves against German and Austrian hostility. As long as the dual alliance remained in existence they felt bound to assume that it perpetuated a secret German hostility against themselves. Russia had to acquiesce rather irritably in the fact that she was losing ground against Austria's economic offensive in the Balkans. But the Tsar would not get rid of the fire-eating generals whose animosity Bismarck feared so unnecessarily. So alarmed did he become at the beginning of 1882 that he decided to form yet another alliance in order this time to prevent or delay an Italian attack on Austria's rear in the event of a Russo–Austrian war; it was also some insurance against France. This was the triple alliance concluded by Germany, Austria, and Italy on 20 May 1882. Serbia was drawn into the alliance network by a secret agreement with Austria in 1881, and Rumania by an agreement in 1883.

This piling up of precautions is impressive in its way. His friendship was valued, Germany's two potential enemies (France and Russia) were kept apart, the Germanic fortress was as diplomatically secure on paper as human ingenuity could make it. And yet he was pessimistic and uneasy, never free from the conviction that only his sleepless vigilance could maintain a balance of animosities among his neighbours and leave him arbiter of the continent. His encouragement of French ambitions in north Africa led to the desired tensions with Italy and England; his support of the impossible ideal of an Austro–Russian division of interests in the Balkan peninsula kept the three emperors' alliance in being for six uneasy years. But it was a highly precarious system, with mounting exasperation everywhere. On the other hand, Gladstone's belief that the rivalries of the continent could be neutralized and dissolved in the warm comradeship of a revived Concert of Europe seemed to him both silly and perverse.

In domestic politics too he had acquired by the early eighties a position of unassailable authority comparable to his standing in Europe, but equally dependent on the balancing of political tensions with, of course, the precious additional asset of the Emperor's continued favour. These were years in which the new political combinations created by the protectionist battle gave him the majorities he needed on critical occasions, although he could take little for granted.

The worries of office might in the circumstances have abated sufficiently to allow him a certain serenity of outlook and relaxation of nervous strain; but in the summer of 1881 he was poorly again, tormented by neuralgia but blaming his exigent master. In January the British ambassador had reported ironically some characteristic repining. 'After his usual complaints about the weary work imposed upon him by the obstinacy of his Imperial Master, the incapacity of his Colleagues, the ignorance of Parliament and the imbecility of mankind, he said that he was glad to rest his weary brain by talking over foreign affairs, which constituted the only recreation in his overworked existence.' Bismarck had forced the Emperor's acceptance of the dual alliance with another threat of resignation in October 1879, but while the old gentleman was willing as usual to give way in the last resort he continued to bombard his imperious servant with peremptory messages, demands, and expostulations. Busch found the Chancellor at the end of June 1881 suffering 'pains all over, in the body, chest, and face'. He claimed that his teeth had been good until his sixty-sixth year (1 April 1881) 'but now they all pain me, tugging and tearing above and below and all round'. He weighed eighteen stone. The beard had appeared again, the usual sign that he was tormented by his 'nervous affection'. And yet, 'the King is pitiless. He knows how ill I am, and yet every day he sends me notes that must be answered'.

What Busch guessed was that Bismarck's condition had been worsened by family troubles. He had recently, with an implacable and no doubt passionate refusal of consent, prevented the marriage of his son Herbert, aged thirty-two, to the countess Carolath-Beuthen, who had secured a divorce in April for the purpose. The lady was the step-sister of Mimi Schleinitz, wife of Alexander von Schleinitz, who as a minister of the Royal Household and former foreign minister had accumulated over the years Bismarck's bitterest dislike. It appears that this, rather than the divorce, explains Bismarck's fierce opposition.

Nor was the course of domestic politics as satisfying as he had hoped. The alliance with the Centre on protection did not lead to their acquiescence in the limited concessions on the Catholic question which he was prepared to offer; they demanded the repeal of the May laws, even although the Pope was ready to accept much less. Bismarck had had to turn once again to the National Liberals in order to secure with Conservative support the renewal of the army law in the summer of 1880. This result was facilitated by an article in the *Norddeutsche Allgemeine Zeitung* which talked of the aggressive attitude of France and Russia, and caused great alarm. But the Liberals disliked even his limited concessions to the Catholics, and the party broke up under the strain. The more prominent leaders, including Lasker, Forckenbeck, and Bamberger, seceded with those of the rank and file who shared their dislike of Bismarck's ideas. So what with the dwindling support of a diminished National Liberal party and with the irreconcilable splinter groups, the representatives of the Polish, Danish, Hanoverian, and Alsatian minorities, voting against him, even the now reliable Conservatives could not give him a regular majority on important questions. But the Centre supported him when it suited their plans to do so.

The last of his great innovations in domestic policy, the programme of social legislation which began in 1881, did appeal to them, while it was thoroughly distasteful to the more extreme Liberals. This programme is his greatest claim to statesmanship in the last decade of his career; for it offered a constructive and imaginative solution of an explosive situation instead of ingeniously perpetuated deadlock as in his foreign policy. Although it was presented with his usual careful attention to timing and parliamentary tactics it expressed broad convictions that he had held since entering politics. He fully shared the paternalistic inclinations of the older Prussian conservatives and of the monarchy, and he had studied in the fifties Napoleon III's skilful employment of universal suffrage, state socialism, and expansive nationalism as a means of winning the support of the masses. In the early days of the constitutional struggle the employment of similar methods had been urged on him by his friend Hermann Wagener. In May 1863 he had started secret talks with Lassalle which went on for ten months, and he rejected the idea of an alliance with the working class parties mainly it would seem because they were quite unrepresentative at this time. His interest in social reform was shown in his efforts in 1864 and 1865 to alleviate the condition of the Silesian weavers who had been hit by the cutting off of raw cotton supplies from the United States, and were being left to endure their lot under the well-established *laissez faire* principles of factory owners and the ministry of the interior. Universal suffrage came in 1867. But what chance there was of a capture of the working class movement by the monarchy was lost during the long era of Liberal predominance that followed. With the passing of the anti-socialist legislation of October 1878 it was too late, although Bismarck did not think so.

The speech from the throne at the opening of the Reichstag in February 1879 called for legislation to remedy social evils, so that the anti-socialist law would be followed by the removal of the legitimate causes of socialism; thus the majority of the proletariat, which had not yet been won over to the 'party of subversion' could still be reconciled to the existing social order. This was explicitly stated by Bismarck to be his aim in April 1881, during the debate on the first accident insurance bill. No doubt he also had in mind the need for a popular platform in the next general election. The Emperor was enthusiastic, and the Conservatives well in accord with plans which fitted their patriarchical and paternalistic conceptions. The Liberals were divided, and drew back with horror from the prospect of state interference with individual freedom. The Centre had long been interested in similar schemes for health insurance, factory legislalation, old age pensions and the like. But they finally objected to the bill as it stood because they considered the employers' contribution too high, and the idea of a state contribution wrong in principle. This was Bismarck's cue to dissolve the Reichstag in November 1881. Unfortunately the magician failed this time to win.

It was with something of a swing back to the older loyalties that the electorate voted heavily for the various Liberal groups, and showed its indifference to the theoretical advantages that social legislation might someday provide. The National Liberal party itself secured only 47 seats, but the Secessionists gained about the same number, while the more intransigent Progressives secured sixty. 'The elections have shown that the German Philistine still lives, and allows himself to be frightened and led astray by fine speeches and lies', was Bismarck's irritated comment. There was momentary talk of resignation, but nothing really to justify it. Until 1887 he was without a dependable majority in the Reichstag, but with the army vote safe for that period he could survive without it.

With declining zest he turned again to accident insurance. A second bill in April 1882 also failed, owing to his continued insistence on state support for the central organization of the scheme; but a sickness insurance bill was introduced at the same time and became law in May 1882, while the accident insurance bill did finally do so in July 1884, after Bismarck had accepted the substance of his critics' proposals. The edifice was revised and strengthened during subsequent years, and a scheme for pensions in cases of old age and infirmity, which had been promised in 1881, was at last introduced in 1888. This was the one which probably interested Bismarck most, and it became law on 22 June 1889, although it was enacted only by his successor. Eugen Richter, the leader of the Progressives, who had denounced the whole programme of state-aided benefit in a shocked voice in April 1881 as 'not socialistic but communistic' had left to the progressive Junker the foundation of the modern welfare state.

Chapter Six

The Last Phase

BY 1884 Bismarck had recovered from many of the mistakes of policy committed during his first years as Chancellor. He changed his mind and with it his policies about as frequently as prime ministers change office in a parliamentary state. No other course was possible if he was to stay in office indefinitely, as the Emperor wished; he had to provide alternative governments to himself. True, his political rivals and possible successors found his presence oppressive and the future depressing, but the public still took him and his plans seriously. It never occurred to him that he was inconsistent, if inconsistency was a sign of incompetence. It was simply that he had acquired a well-merited position which enabled him to make necessary changes of course. Nor would he agree that the range of courses was arbitrary and narrow.

He was getting old, and the Emperor ever older. Foreign diplomats gleefully reported any signs of decrepitude. He said from time to time that he would like to retire after the old Emperor's death; perhaps there were moments when office palled and he really meant it. But against this had to be set his dark thoughts of the disaster that would inevitably descend on the Reich with his incompetent successors. So he stayed in office, on the alert to canalize the anger or ambition or mere restlessness of troublemakers at home and abroad. The towering figure towered ever higher in the eyes of his admiring countrymen. On his seventieth birthday (1 April 1885) he was presented with a large sum, about £270,000, raised by public subscription. He gave some to charity, and used the rest to repurchase the estate of Schönhausen. 'The eighties elevated the great Chancellor and his aged Emperor to a great eminence' wrote Erich Marcks in 1902, 'and Prince Bismarck, the Prussian, was then, both in reality and in the people's heart, the embodiment of the new Germany. He became in the deepest sense a spiritual force for his people.'

There was, however, little that was noticeably spiritual in his domestic policy during his last years of office. He seemed to forget about social legislation for a time, and to be in no hurry to complete the liquidation of the *Kulturkampf*. Foreign affairs took up his attention more and more, and warnings as to mounting dangers from abroad rallied the faithful once again to the support of the Fatherland. He now moved almost exclusively in the orbit of Berlin–Varzin–Friedrichsruh, never going abroad, rarely visiting any other parts of Germany. He seemed to have no aim beyond the indefinite continuation of the favourable balance of things as they were. Opposition as usual made him angry and vindictive, and from one point of view his public activity was little more than a series of personal battles, sometimes injudiciously chosen, with much misunderstood adversaries. Even his admirers were uneasy at his habit of staging the public discomfiture of his opponents, even in the royal circle, instead of trying to win them over in private. Holstein regarded this as the prime mistake of Bismarck's last crisis, preceding his resignation in March 1890.

For these last years of continued strain he was unexpectedly revitalized by an improvement in health. Persistent over-eating combined with the nervous irritability which had agitated and upset him since the late fifties had produced a fearsome list of complaints, which he would rather piteously recount on occasion. They were partly imaginary, partly induced, but partly genuine. His doctors had hitherto been quite unable to impose their own ideas of treatment on him. Dr. Struck had given up the uneven struggle in June 1881. In the spring of 1883 Bismarck seemed so doddery and weak, able to totter along only with a walking stick because of the severe pains in his legs, that medical opinion privately gave him only a year to live.

Just at this point Dr. Schweninger, not yet 33 years old, took over. He had made an impression on the family by curing Bismarck's second son Wilhelm of gout by a strict diet, but some time was to elapse before Bismarck gave him a trial. Devoted and autocratic, he not only bullied his illustrious patient into following a sparse and nutritious diet, but by some strange and soothing therapeutic feat gave him for a time the boon of deep and regular sleep. In a surprisingly short time Bismarck seemed a new man. When Lucius von Ballhausen visited him in December 1883 he was lean, robust, free from pain, able to take long walks again. The diet continued, and with it the improvement. Moritz Busch found him 'quite young and rosy' in February 1885. Eating herrings on Schweninger's recommendation he estimated in 1888 that he had disposed of over a thousand.

Until the autumn of 1885 the foreign situation remained sufficiently quiescent for him to feel satisfied with his control of European tensions. Domestic politics were rather more troublesome. We have seen that the 1881 elections had left the Centre party, skilfully led by the sardonic and watchful Windthorst, holding the balance between the pro-Bismarckian and anti-Bismarckian groups. The Conservatives and the small National Liberal party were not sufficient to give him a majority. The social legislation did not now seem likely to tilt the party balance much in his favour in the Reichstag. In the spring of 1884 the Secessionist Liberals united with the Progressives to form the German Radical, 'Deutsch-Freisinnigen', Party, thus presenting the regime with a united Liberal opposition of a hundred members.

He was naturally disposed in the circumstances to do something for the business and protectionist circles and pick up some popularity for them and for himself, and the growing colonial movement offered opportunities for this, although he had produced sage and apparently incontrovertible arguments against a colonial policy in the past. These faithful echoes of Frederician isolationism, stressing the need to concentrate strength in Europe, were not abandoned; at any rate, he still declared at intervals until his retirement that he was no 'colonial man'. He nevertheless acquired a sizeable colonial empire for Germany, and a sizeable quarrel with Gladstone at the same time. Historians have never been quite agreed as to Bismarck's real motives for this new turn of policy, for it can be argued that it was any one of several, or several at once. He could expect some real help to German industry from the encouragement of trade, some political advantages at home through the satisfaction of a popular demand, a basis for co-operation with France, the emotional satisfaction of some sharp words with Gladstone, and the discrediting of English influences in the Crown Prince's entourage. Which were the main, and which the secondary objectives?

As in all his major enterprises, he felt able to control his commitments precisely; it is a reasonable deduction from his subsequent course that he meant the colonial activity to go on only as long as it helped, or did not interfere with, the other ends of home and foreign policy. But his unhappy inability to push through his clever manoeuvres without making himself thoroughly unpleasant in the process was once more displayed. After the Austrians, French, and Russians it was now the turn of the British.

All the evidence goes to show that he was developing a colonial policy long before any question of a quarrel with England arose in the summer of 1884. Enterprising German traders had been receiving the support of the German Foreign Office since the first years of the empire. Companies were developing trade with Zanzibar and the west coast of Africa, and a Hamburg merchant, Godeffroy, had since 1860 been building up a position of great strength in Samoa and the south Pacific islands. Missionary activity had also given the Germans a number of footholds, particularly in south-west Africa and some Pacific islands. From about the mid-seventies organized demands for the acquisition of colonies began to be heard from business and shipping interests in the northern ports, Hamburg and Bremen, and in the Rhineland. Financial support came from the Berlin Discount Company. Bismarck was in no hurry to act but he told the Bremen merchant Lüderitz in 1876 that he was favourable to colonial development as soon as the nation was ready for it.

The turn to protection in 1879 was accompanied by a rapid abandonment of *laissez faire* ideas in every field. Such incidents as his support of German economic interests in Rumania in 1878–9 and a sudden public condemnation of the Khedive of Egypt's financial conduct in May 1879 (assumed in London to have been instigated by Bleichröder on behalf of German bondholders) revealed a growing preoccupation with the possibilities of state aid to his business friends. When Godeffroy's firm got into difficulties later in 1879 Bismarck came to the rescue with a financial guarantee, in order to frustrate a British take-over bid. But his Samoan Subsidy bill was defeated in the Reichstag in April 1880 as a result of fierce Liberal opposition, supported by the Centre and the socialists. Apart from the strong doctrinaire objection to colonization which Bismarck himself had necessarily accepted during the years of his Liberal alliance, the Liberals were bound to treat the proffered help as a gift from public funds to a powerful supporter of the regime.

But popular interest was growing; books and pamphlets, extolling the economic advantages of colonies, multiplied, and the civilizing mission was not forgotten. A colonial society, the *Kolonialverein*, was founded in 1882, followed by another, the Association for German Colonization, in 1884. Membership of the *Kolonialverein* went up rapidly, and its propaganda was pushed vigorously among businessmen and officials, as well as in the universities. There was also much resistance to these proposals however. Bismarck never was an 'imperialist' in the sense of desiring to build a large navy, or a colonial army, or a system of alliances directed against the British Empire.

The publicity value of a colonial policy played a large part in his plans, and he did not seem to have thought out what he meant by the 'protection' of German merchants in Africa or the southern Pacific, and similar gestures.

His various activities in African questions do seem, however, to have been part of a single coherent policy. In 1880 he supported the French against the British over Morocco, in 1881 he cordially approved the French protectorate over Tunis, in and after July 1882 he supported the British government diplomatically against the French in matters arising from the British occupation of Egypt. In August 1881 on the other hand a German warship was dispatched to South-West Africa on the request of German missionaries for protection. In November 1882 Lüderitz had been promised by Bismarck a 'limited protection' if he should acquire territory for a factory in South-West Africa not claimed by any other power. Even the unsuspicious Odo Russell warned Granville, the British foreign secretary, on 9 May 1883, that Bismarck might soon press German claims strongly in Fiji and elsewhere, in order to show Germany that he could protect German interests all over the world.

Probably, however, he had not yet decided how popular feeling could best be exploited and it was the apparent determination of British interests, acting through Granville, to thwart him over his plans for south-west Africa that made the Angra Pequena question the main issue. There were several enquiries about British claims to the bleak coast of south-west Africa. They did not want the trouble of occupying it, but thought they had a better claim to do so than anyone else. On 31 December 1883 a long German dispatch asked for precise information as to the British grounds for such claims, and Derby, the colonial minister, still under the impression that Bismarck did not want colonies, embarked on leisurely discussions with the Cape government on the matter. So Bismarck was kept waiting for six months, and as late as 2 June 1884 the colonial office was still talking in terms of obliging Bismarck by affording protection for German merchants.

It is possible to see in these German activities a deliberate attempt to lead the amiable British statesmen up the garden path, and this view has been taken by Erich Eyck and some of Bismarck's other critics. Odo Russell (who died on 24 August 1884) continued to assure his government that Bismarck did not want colonies. The German ambassador in London, Count Münster, said more or less the same, and gave no hint of a change of policy or of any great urgency. On 17 May he rather coyly mentioned to Granville the possibility of the cession of Heligoland by Britain to Germany, following what he thought were Bismarcks' instructions in a despatch of 5 May. On 25 May a telegram from Bismarck instructed Münster not to mention Heligoland further; Angra Pequena was still not mentioned, and it was not until yet another despatch of 1 June that Münster was at last informed explicitly that this was what now mainly interested Bismarck. It was not, however, until Herbert Bismarck, who had been first secretary to the embassy in London since 1882, started talks on 14 June that Granville at last understood the position.

Can one accuse Bismarck of duplicity towards Britain in his handling of the Angra Pequena issue? What useful purpose would duplicity have served? None certainly during May, when he was still sending Münster long but rather cryptic messages at intervals from Friedrichsruh. It seems much more probable that since the beginning of 1884 he was in a state of somewhat irritable indecision on the colonial issue, owing first to his lack of detailed knowledge of colonial matters and their possible pitfalls, and secondly to a growing resentment against the British, who were not making things easy for him. His tendency to plunge into vindictive and unprofitable counter-measures in such circumstances was by now familiar enough. Colonial successes would be useful to him politically, and an anti-English campaign would be popular; but it is doubtful if his action during the next six months was due merely to such cool calculation. He felt himself thwarted;

for years he had indulged in derisory comments on Liberalism in general and Gladstone in particular; England was isolated in 1884 as Russia had been in 1879, and he could safely work off much accumulated irritation against her. As usual, his tactical manoeuvres were entirely successful. But once again he created a basic hostility which had not existed before, and which could not be forgotten when he changed his tune. He could have secured his ends at much less emotional cost—to himself and others—if he had studied the problem more thoroughly and expressed himself more clearly. Despatches during the crisis were drafted by the anglophobe Lothar Bucher, who always rejoiced in Britain's discomfiture. Germany had no colonial office. Von Küsserow, the capable head of the commercial department of the Foreign Office, does not seem to have been consulted.

It was in this mood that Bismarck decided to embark on a colonial policy, deliberately challenging British interests at each stage, and with increasing reliance on French support for the next six months. On 24 April he telegraphed to Cape Town his decision, already privately communicated to Lüderitz on 14 March, to annex the settlement at Angra Pequena. At the same time he arranged for Dr. Nachtigal to go to the Cameroons and asked the British authorities in the area to give him assistance; this Granville agreed to do, after being assured that Nachtigal's interests were commercial and scientific, not political. Duplicity again? On 19 May Nachtigal was instructed to annex the Cameroons in spite of British interests in the area, although he was to be scrupulously careful not to encroach on French interests. The British consul, Hewitt, was not in time to forestall Nachtigal in the Cameroons, where the local chiefs wanted British protection, but he was able to safeguard the British position in the Niger delta. Bismarck also renewed earlier demands by German settlers in Fiji for compensation, and organized an expedition under the auspices of a newly-formed German New Guinea Company to see what could be picked up in this island which Australia wanted to control.

After Granville had learned from Herbert Bismarck what his father really wanted the British cabinet agreed on 21 June to recognize the German protectorate at Angra Pequena. On 19 June a mixed commission was appointed to examine the Fiji claims. In accordance with his instructions, which he carried out with some truculence, Herbert had threatened the withdrawal of German support over Egypt. These concessions came just in time for Bismarck to use them effectively in the Budget Commission of the Reichstag, and to triumph over Bamberger and Richter. They also had a favourable reception in the German press. Bismarck saw no reason why he should not push on with his wider policy of expansion, with French help. The six months delay in answering his questions about Angra Pequena had led him to the conclusion that the forceful course would be more profitable than the alternative one of bargaining for concessions from the British in return for his support over Egypt. The last straw, and final confirmation of his suspicions, came when Derby, assuming that German claims were limited to the areas adjacent to Angra Pequena, arranged on 16 July for the Cape Colony to annex Bechuanaland and those parts of the coast of south-west Africa not already occupied by Lüderitz. A conference which sat in London from 28 June to 2 August to deal with Egyptian finance made the breach public. Bismarck, who first heard of Derby's action through the newspapers, was furious. He refused to recognize the decision; declared a German protectorate over the whole coastline from the Portuguese border to the Orange river, and joined the other powers in refusing the British proposals over the disposal of the Egyptian revenue. He then completed plans for joint action with France.

The occasion for this was provided by the Anglo-Portuguese treaty of 26 February 1884, which he thoroughly misunderstood. The Portuguese, with vague but ancient claims to the Congo region, were fearful of French ex-

pansion in the area and consequent high tariffs; finding
the British government in the same mood, they signed the
treaty in order to keep the French out, and not to let the
British in. The British government had no designs on the
Congo; they had declined to recognize the annexation of
the Congo basin on their behalf by Lieutenant V. L.
Cameron in 1875. They preferred the Portuguese to the
more formidable French. Britain insisted in the treaty on
absolute freedom of transit for goods inland, but she
accepted after much argument the Portuguese plan for
an Anglo-Portuguese commission for the river, although
she would have preferred an international commission.
After the French and other powers had made objections
to the treaty Bismarck proposed to Ferry in May that
France and Germany should insist on the reference of the
Congo question to an international conference with free
trade and navigation and an international commission
as a basis. On 14 June he refused to recognize the treaty,
quite sure now that he was frustrating British ambitions.
In August he proposed to Ferry a far-reaching entente
whereby Germany should support French aims in Egypt,
and France should support German plans in West Africa,
including the Congo.

The French at first did not know what to make of all
this, for it was they who, in the Congo and elsewhere,
were the pacemakers. They agreed that there should be
freedom of trade on the Congo coast, free navigation of
the river, and an international commission. But they jibbed
at Bismarck's proposal to extend the principle of freedom
of commerce to any parts of the African coast that either
might occupy in future; their practice was to keep foreign
trade out of their colonies by high tariffs. Even Bismarck's
offer to limit free trade to regions south of the equator
did not satisfy them, and they insisted that the rule should
be confined to the Congo basin. They were also uneasy
about the sweeping nature of Bismarck's conditions for
effective occupation, which might obviously work to their
own disadvantage. The British, who were confirmed free
traders with no desire to be embarrassed by further com-

mitments and protectorates, were quite willing to leave things as they were; it was only when other powers seemed likely to seize areas where they had long-standing trading interests or which might threaten communications with India that they were driven to counter-action.

Thus there was nothing in Bismarck's general conditions to which they need object; and they were more bewildered by his gratuitous hostility (as they saw it) than ever. They had great difficulty in getting any explanation from him as to his proposals for the Congo conference. When it met its result was, unexpectedly, something of a triumph for them. Neither Britain nor Germany wanted to annex the Congo area, for its trade was not sufficient to interest them; but Britain also wanted very much to keep the French out, and this result she secured, with Bismarck's almost unwitting help. She also secured acceptance by the conference and by Bismarck of her dominant position on the lower Niger, and she successfully opposed Bismarck's attempt to give the conditions for effective occupation too rigid a definition. The chief beneficiary of the Congo negotiations was King Leopold of Belgium, who skilfully made use of the divisions of the powers and Bismarck's suspicions of the British to secure the recognition of his own international Association as the ruler of the area.

Bismarck was evidently coming to the reluctant conclusion before the end of the conference in January 1885 that there were no real grounds of difference between him and the British, although he continued to stage periodic explosions as a prelude to fresh colonial demands until his retirement in 1890. Meanwhile he found to his embarrassment that colonies could be expensive and unprofitable, particularly in inexpert hands. But although he had reason to seek British diplomatic support in other fields after Salisbury had succeeded Gladstone in 1886 he did not entirely abandon this quarrelsome attitude, and the fact that he had deliberately chosen his colonial acquisitions in areas that would annoy them most made a complete reconciliation impossible. Not that he gained

anything from his flirtation with the French. The disaster
to French arms in Tonkin in March 1885 led to Ferry's
defeat, and a wave of apprehension among Frenchmen
over the diversion of strength from the Rhine. A new
phase of anti-German feeling was soon to show that
Bismarck had achieved little with his policy of reconciliation towards France since 1877.

Home colonization in the shape of an attempt to ger-
manize Prussia's Polish provinces also took an aggressive
form at this time. Bismarck's alarm at the nationalist spirit
among the Poles had been revealed in 1863, and it continued to agitate him. Given equality of opportunity the
Polish farmer did better than his German neighbour, and
it was believed that the Polish population was increasing
at twice the rate of the German. On the other hand he
regarded the Polish aristocracy and clergy as the real
enemies of Germany, while the masses, mainly agricultural peasantry, seemed acquiescent and loyal; their re-
cruits had fought well in the three wars. The first offensive against the Polish position had been the *Kulturkampf*, and the privileged position of the Roman church
as a rallying ground for Polish disloyalty had been proclaimed as one of the major targets of the struggle. The
second was advocated by Robert von Puttkamer, a strong
conservative, related to Bismarck's wife. He had succeeded
Falk as Prussian *Kultusminister* in 1879, and was minister
of the interior from 1881 to 1888.

Bismarck is said to have had some reluctance to act in
this case, just as he is said to have agreed to the *Kulturkampf* and the colonial policy with reservations. In all
three cases the hesitations were on grounds of tactics rather
than of principle, and he was finally persuaded by Puttkamer and others that there were reasonable chances of
success and a compelling need. Accordingly an edict of 5
May 1885 expelled all Poles who were not legally Prussian
subjects; this got rid of 34,000, and in the following year
an expropriation bill was carried in the Landtag to provide for the buying up of Polish estates for leasing to

German farmers. The farmers were to be compelled to marry German wives. In a curious and rather passionate speech Bismarck justified these plans, which were to cost an initial five million pounds, on the ground that Germans abroad had an extraordinary tendency 'to sympathize with everything that was not German'.

Thus began a struggle which further advertised the tendency to ultimate violence in Bismarck's policies, and which failed as the *Kulturkampf* had failed. There were critics of the policy in Germany, but the Prussian Landtag agreed wholeheartedly with the programme, and Bismarck refused to recognize the problem as one within the jurisdiction of the Reichstag. The supervision of popular education was also placed in the hands of the Prussian Settlement Commission. The Poles had now to struggle for their religion, language, culture, and livelihood. In fact, they held their own extremely well. They were more prolific than the Germans. German settlers and farmers continued to be forced back by keener agricultural techniques, supported by a well-organized communal co-operative system. The struggle continued with mounting severity after Bismarck's retirement. The deliberate choice of repressive methods gave Bismarck another black mark in history, although no one could say that more conciliatory or quiescent methods would have prevented the real danger of a quite rapid polonization of German territory.

The colonial activity was probably of some help to Bismarck in the Reichstag elections in the autumn of 1884. The Radical Liberals lost more than a third of their seats, while the Conservatives increased theirs by a half. But the Socialists gained 24 seats, doubling their numbers, and vastly increasing their electoral support, and although the Centre could give Bismarck a majority when they combined with the Conservatives they did not always choose to do so. They did not like his colonial policy, and they had not yet secured the repeal of all the anti-Catholic legislation.

But his main preoccupation as Chancellor from 1885 to 1888 was the threat to European peace and to his system of alliances from the bellicose attitudes of Russia and France. The elaborate network of alliances which he had built up had been reassuring as long as Europe was quiescent; but as the purpose was to save Germany from involvement in other people's problems any attempt by an ally to secure his support was embarrassing and had to be skilfully evaded. The result was negotiation on two levels : ostensibly an effort to find a peaceful solution of explosive problems, lest worst befall; under cover of this, secret assurances to both sides in order to retain the good-will of both if peace ensued. What would have happened if war had broken out is one of the most curious problems of modern diplomacy.

The distinctive quality of Bismarck's diplomacy since 1871 had been his substitution of a balance of tensions for the balance of power. The aim of the balance of power had been to strengthen the security, and therefore the sense of security, of individual states by massing strength against a possible aggressor. Bismarck now wished above all things to keep Germany out of war. It was obviously an advantage, which he hardly troubled to conceal, that Russia should find her attention absorbed in wrangles with the Austrians or Turks in the Balkans or with the British in Asia Minor and Central Asia; or that the French should pursue an imperial path which turned their attention away from Alsace-Lorraine to Africa and Indo-China, to the progressive annoyance of Italy, Great Britain, and the Chinese Empire. It would also be an advantage to have established himself in their view as a sympathetic friend, and possibly an ally or mediator; their differences with Germany would be pushed into the background and he would be able to exert influence and prevent crises getting out of hand. But this programme was really a gigantic exercise in wishful thinking. It was rather too much to expect his neighbours to bicker indefinitely with one another, never agreeing and yet never overstepping the mark, in order to preserve his peace of mind.

The system broke down at its first challenge. No one trusted him very far. The Russian diplomat Jomini called him the Minotaur. His reputation as a diplomat cardsharper had been thoroughly established in the sixties; the seventies had convinced France and Russia of his underlying hostility, in spite of later conciliatory gestures; his desire to score off the Gladstone government made the British wary of 'blackmail'. The Austrians and Italians did not fear his hostility, but were doubtful whether they could benefit much from his support. All these relations were put to the test with the outbreak of a fresh crisis in the Balkans, and the three emperors' alliance speedily collapsed. He was still trying to patch up the alliance structure at the time of his fall from office in 1890.

The three emperors' alliance was renewed without change in 1884, but only after Giers had remarked to the Russian ambassadors in 1883 that its sole value was to neutralize German hostility. When Saburov tried to make the renewal of the treaty the occasion for genuine gains for Russia, Bismarck said that he had lost confidence in the sanguine ambassador's judgment, and he was recalled. The new crisis followed the decision of Bulgaria and the Turkish province of Eastern Rumelia to unite themselves under Prince Alexander of Bulgaria on 18 September 1885. Alexander III had developed a great hatred for the young man and accordingly Russia, to everyone's astonishment, opposed the union. Although Austria and Germany dutifully supported their ally Russia and the Turks in demanding the restoration of the Bulgarian *status quo*, the Tsar was suspicious of their attitude, particularly when Kálnoky, the Austrian foreign minister, seemed to be taking advantage of the crisis to push Serbian interests. However, Bismarck did succeed in persuading Kálnoky for a time to render lip service to the alliance, and to leave the British government, which had energetically supported Prince Alexander, to bear the brunt of Russian annoyance. Things took a turn for the worse a year later after the prince, having made no headway with the Russians, abdicated, and the uncompromising Bulgarian premier, Stambulov, nevertheless stoutly resisted the Russian government's attempt to reimpose its influence. The Tsar broke off diplomatic relations with Bulgaria in November 1886.

Was this to be the prelude to a Russian invasion and occupation of Bulgaria? Austrian and British hostility to any such intervention could not be concealed. The crisis was not due, however, merely to personal tension between the Tsar and his ungrateful Bulgarian protégés. Sensible politicians like Giers saw no profit for Russia in Panslavism, and no hopes of economic dominance in the peninsula in the face of Austrian competition. Even in Bulgaria they had retained an economic footing only by exclusive tactics which had turned the Bulgarians against them. To this group all that really mattered was that the Straits should be kept out of British hands. But prestige and the Tsar's anger made it impossible to write off the Balkans in this way, and it seemed possible all through 1887 that there might be a Russian attack followed by a great war in the Near East.

In the meantime, however, Bismarck had three other problems. He was still pushing on with his colonial acquisitions in Africa, and although he found it expedient to treat Salisbury, British prime minister after July 1886, rather more circumspectly than he had handled Gladstone, there were inevitable clashes. The rapid rise of General Boulanger in France and the possibility (which Bismarck probably did not take very seriously) of a French attack, gave an excellent opportunity to bring in a new army bill, but this would need some accentuation of Franco–German tension and it might bring France and Russia together. Thirdly there was the problem of renewing the triple alliance in view of the dissatisfaction of both Italy and Austria with its terms : Italy wanted support against France for her Mediterranean policy, and Austria demanded German and Italian support against Russia in the Balkans. A collapse of his two tripartite alliances, a choice between Russia and Austria, a possible war with

France—all the complications that his system was planned to avoid—were threatened by this combination of crises.

His solution was to abandon the balance-of-tensions policy for balance-of-power diplomacy on the more traditional model, which would not have disgraced Metternich. It was a curious game in which Bismarck made the rules. There was systematic duplicity, in the form of assurances and encouragements to each side which had to be concealed from the other; there was also some calculated publicity, and he managed to dictate as to when secrecy should or should not apply. In the same way he had sought to disconcert Gladstone by diplomatic revelations while objecting bitterly to any blue book publications which embarrassed himself. His admirers patiently reiterate that all this is a miracle of sophisticated diplomacy. We may spare a moment for the thought that the old gentleman had slightly lost his head. Germany's influence, which was due to her natural strength and lack of territorial ambition in Europe, did not require these complicated subterfuges. They could not be entirely concealed, and they created a constant and unnecessary suspicion as to his intentions.

He scored a complete domestic triumph over the army bill, with a complex campaign designed ostensibly to guarantee long-term planning, but in fact to strengthen his hold on the Reichstag. In view of the European tensions in 1886 there was no opposition to the strengthening of the army by 10 per cent as Bismarck demanded; he was satisfied that owing to heavier expenditure and a more rigorous system of recruitment the French peacetime establishment under the system of national conscription was ahead of that of Germany. Under the seven years' legislation the arrangement of 1881 was not due to expire until April 1888; the introduction of a new bill more than a year earlier was thus a means of emphasizing the gravity of the international situation. The Centre and the Progressives however were prepared to agree only to a three-year term. The Catholic leaders thus ignored direct instructions from the Pope to support the bill.

When defeat was certain, Bismarck rose on 11 January 1887 and delivered an impressive oration to the Reichstag in which he affirmed his belief in the pacific inclinations of all the European governments, assured Russia that the Austro–German alliance did not commit Germany to the support of Austrian plans in the Balkans, and made it clear that the military bill was directed only against a possible threat from France. Von Moltke, the aged Chief of Staff, made a memorable appearance before the Reichstag and asserted that rejection meant war. In spite of these rumblings from on high, the bill was defeated, the Reichstag was promptly dissolved on 14 January, and after a fierce campaign of denunciation of French intentions in the government press, a handsome victory was secured for the government parties in the elections on 21 February. The bill was then passed by a large majority in the new Reichstag on 11 March, with eighty-three of Windthorst's ninety supporters refraining from voting. The opposition Liberals and the Socialists had lost heavily, and the government parties—the two Conservative groups and the National Liberals—secured 220 out of 297 seats. They combined under the name of the *Kartell* to give Bismarck a safe majority in the Reichstag for the next three years.

He could now turn to the building up of the system of precautions which was to restrain France and Russia from their somewhat problematical courses of aggression. Although the flamboyant Boulanger continued to excite chauvinistic sentiments in some parts of the French press, the French cabinet seems to have been peacefully inclined throughout, and Bismarck now showed that he had little doubt on the point. The potentially dangerous Schnaebele incident was settled without fuss in April 1887, and ultimately the French found means of eliminating Boulanger. It was a longer task to mollify the Russians, who were angry with the Germans without being quite sure why. The powerful Moscow journalist Michael Katkov, encouraged by some revelations from the disgruntled Saburov, violently attacked the three emperors' alliance

as an unfair bargain for Russia, while other Russian
journalists made outright demands for a Franco–Russian
alliance. The Tsar was obviously influenced for a time,
and French diplomats received from the Russians encouraging messages in January and February 1887. But
Katkov overreached himself, Giers regained Alexander's
ear, and in March it was decided to work for a separate
agreement with Germany. Alexander was adamant in
refusing to consider a renewal of the three emperors'
alliance.

The result, after rather difficult negotiations, was the
so-called reinsurance treaty signed on 18 June 1887, the
day that the three emperors' alliance expired. The term
'reinsurance' is usually regarded as a description of Bismarck's attempt to bolster his own position, but it was
even more applicable to Russia's attitude. The clauses
show that Germany's position was drastically weakened
as compared with that of 1881. For the three emperors'
alliance had been based in Article 1 on the undertaking
that each of the three would maintain a benevolent neutrality if one of the other two 'found itself at war' with a
fourth power. Thus Russia would be neutral in a Franco–
German war, but Germany did not undertake to be neutral in an Austro–Russian war. The Russians now insisted
on complete reciprocity, and as the Austro–German
alliance prevented Germany from promising neutrality
in all circumstances in an Austro–Russian war, Russia
was not prepared to stand aside in a Franco–German war.
So the first article of the new treaty had to be simply a
pledge of benevolent neutrality which would not apply
either to a Franco–German or an Austro–Russian war :
clearly a worsening of Germany's position.

The rest of the treaty contained Germany's promise to
recognize the preponderant and decisive influence of
Russia in Bulgaria, no essential change from 1881 ; and to
accept a Russian seizure of the Straits or Constantinople.
It was a secret treaty, and the secret was not revealed to
the Austrians or even to the Emperor Frederick when he
came to the throne in 1888. William II claimed to have

been told about it only after Bismarck's dismissal. It was to last for three years. An 'additional and very secret protocol' contained Bismarck's promise to aid Russia in reestablishing a regular and legal government in Bulgaria and to give moral and diplomatic support if Russia should 'assume the task of defending the entrance of the Black Sea'.

So Germany had promised her approval and moral support to Russia in a war arising out of the Bulgarian question and involving the seizure of the Straits. But Bismarck had made the same promise of support to Russia's potential opponents, also in highly secret terms. The circumstances which led him into this equivocal position were not entirely under his control. Up to the end of 1886 he had still had hopes of saving the three emperors' alliance and had continued to urge Kálnoky to lie low and leave Salisbury to bear the brunt of Russian animosity. But Kálnoky and Salisbury, although each professing doubts as to the other's seriousness of purpose, were convinced that some agreement to face a Russian offensive was necessary. At the same time France was alarming both England and Italy by her Mediterranean activities, and on 12 February 1887 Salisbury and Robilant, the Italian foreign minister, exchanged letters undertaking to work together in support of the *status quo* in the Mediterranean, Adriatic, Aegean, and Black Seas. By giving his blessing to this agreement and treating it as a supplement to the triple alliance, Bismarck was able to persuade Italy and Austria to renew the alliance (20 February 1887), and on 24 March Salisbury and Kálnoky also exchanged notes undertaking to support the *status quo* in lands bordering on the Mediterranean. Bismarck had shown ingenuity in bringing about the renewal of the triple alliance by these means, but he would presumably have preferred an Austro–Russian reconciliation.

The reinsurance treaty seemed for a moment to have swung his support to Russia's side, and he collaborated with her in Constantinople for some weeks; but by the autumn of 1887 the continued criticisms of Germany in the Russian press and some evidence of renewed military preparations agitated him again, and led to several ostentatious anti-Russian gestures. At the same time he encouraged the Mediterranean group to draw up closer agreements (completed in December 1887). Russia again began to feel German diplomatic pressure at Constantinople, and on 10 November the Reichsbank was forbidden to accept Russian securities as collateral for loans. This was no doubt considered a clever means of pressure, but it misfired; German businessmen hurriedly got rid of their Russian securities, and these were largely bought up by the French, with a profit of some 500 million francs. Alexander III's attitude was shown a week later, when he visited Berlin. Copies of letters, almost certainly forged, had come into his hands implicating Bismarck in Prince Ferdinand of Coburg's efforts to seize the Bulgarian throne. The Tsar made it clear that he would accept the denials of Emperor William, but not of Bismarck.

When we contemplate these strange alternations of policy we can hardly praise Bismarck even for successful duplicity. The peaceful turn in Russian policy had come in the spring of 1887 with the decision to seek a German and not a French alliance and although the Mediterranean grouping may have been a necessary precaution it cannot be said to have been the cause of this decision. The value of the reinsurance treaty lay in the fact that if the touchy and suspicious Russians could be assured that they had a reliable friend they could hope to disentangle themselves from their Balkan embarrassments without too much loss of face. Bismarck's habit of giving his friends smart raps over the knuckles at frequent intervals in order to remind them of his importance might be merely annoying, or it might arouse—as in this case—the suspicion that his policy had changed. But the capacity to disconcert, which he had been displaying with so much virtuosity ever since 1862, was now combined with a fear of risks, so that his diplomacy was at once irritating and unadventurous.

In April 1887 Salisbury in his turn was exasperated by

a sudden demand for the dismissal of a young British vice-consul in Zanzibar who had incurred the Chancellor's remote wrath by his allegedly tactless behaviour. A loyal and obstinate man, Salisbury objected strongly to such bullying, and was rewarded with the prompt suspension of German support over the Egyptian negotiations in Constantinople. The vice-consul was moved after a suitable interval to a better appointment. 'The Chancellor's humours are as changeable as those of the French Assembly' wrote Salisbury a year later, 'and you never can be certain that he will not try to levy a sort of diplomatic blackmail.' And yet he was satisfied that Bismarck's fundamental purpose, in spite of his tortuous methods, was peace. The Bulgarian crisis died down in the spring of 1888, leaving Bismarck as worried as ever about French and Russian intentions, yet determined to maintain the bridge to St. Petersburg.

Domestic politics during these last years of his chancellorship were as trying to his temper and his nerves as were foreign relations, and yet no obvious loss of popularity can be detected until perhaps the last weeks. As long as the old Emperor, who was obviously failing after an illness in 1885, was alive, Bismarck's position was secure. Germany and the world continued to accept the great monolithic figure of the Chancellor at very much his own valuation. His more irritable reactions and less dignified expedients were largely concealed from the public. The aloof, Olympian quality was accentuated by his continued long absences in his northern retreats and by the complexities of the constitutional structure of the empire. The citizen's day-to-day contacts were with the rules and regulations and officials of the state governments. Even in Prussia Bismarck as prime minister did not receive the same degree of individual blame for administrative blunders as, for example, the prime minister of the United Kingdom. Occasionally on great public occasions, such as his set speeches to the Reichstag on 11 January 1887 or 6 February 1888, the onlookers were privileged to gaze with awe on the vast uniformed figure of the statesman, who always rose to the occasion with some fine phrases. 'We can easily be corrupted by love and good will—perhaps too easily—but by threats, absolutely not! We Germans fear God and nothing else in the world.' The Bismarck legend was firmly established.

His political success over the army bill in 1887 was of great importance to him in the forthcoming struggle for power. Anticipating it he had moved his son Herbert, aged 36, to the secretaryship of state for foreign affairs in May 1886. The death of the Emperor would be followed by the reign of the Crown Prince Frederick, a liberally inclined but somewhat indecisive man in spite of his fine presence, adorned by a heavy beard. His wife, Victoria, the able and dedicated but rather insensitive eldest daughter of Queen Victoria, was firmly fixed in Bismarck's mind as a menace to his interests. He was sure that she would nag her husband when the chance came into a Liberal policy and a 'Gladstone government'. Since the Radicals were so favoured by the two as to be known popularly as the 'Crown Prince's party', there seemed good reason to believe that with their 67 seats and the support of the Centre and some smaller oppositional groups they might be able to provide the Crown Prince with a cabinet when he succeeded. By deliberately inflating the war scare and by making an issue of the three-year term for the military budget to which the Radicals were pledged, Bismarck as we have seen decisively weakened the party in the general election in February 1887. With the *Kartell* to support him he could be satisfied that Frederick would not be able to find the elements of a 'Gladstone cabinet' for the next three years.

The anti-Socialist law had been renewed in February 1886 for two years, in accordance with a compromise proposal by the Centre. On 17 February 1888 Bismarck, now assured of the *Kartell's* support, secured the passing of a new bill extending the anti-socialist legislation until 30 September 1890. Meanwhile the negotiations over the army bill had prepared the way for the final end of the

Kulturkampf. Bismarck had been tempting the Pope with conciliatory gestures since the early eighties, and earned a decoration for his tact in asking Leo XIII to arbitrate in the Caroline islands dispute in 1885. Earlier Baron von Schlözer had been sent to Rome to reopen diplomatic relations, and had himself been appointed German envoy. From the end of 1883 deposed bishops were being restored to their dioceses, and the payment of state stipends was resumed in all dioceses by the beginning of 1885. Looking for the final end of the *Kulturkampf* and German help against the Italian government, Leo ordered the Centre to throw its whole weight on the government's side in the Septennat struggle, and was displeased at Windthorst's refusal, in January 1887, although the party did not feel able to persist in its revolt. A bill to end the *Kulturkampf* was later introduced into the Prussian Landtag and in supporting it and reviewing the struggle in a speech of 23 March 1887 Bismarck was able to speak with satisfaction of the settlement, and of the Pope's support, which had destroyed the alliance of the Centre with the Radicals. Thus he had prepared his position with care for the imminent struggle to dominate a new master with, perhaps, dangerous—anglophil and Liberal—ideas.

But he had, in fact, prepared for the wrong fight. He had anticipated a struggle with the Liberals. But when the old Emperor died on 9 March 1888 his son was already doomed. Frederick had cancer of the throat when he came to the throne in March and he died in June. He continued Bismarck in office. This did not prevent what seems in the circumstances a somewhat unnecessary campaign of self-assertion on Bismarck's part. Frederick had proposed to reinstate Prince Alexander of Battenberg in the German army and there were plans for him to marry the new Emperor's daughter (another Victoria). In April Bismarck launched a violent campaign in the press against the Empress and Queen Victoria, hinted at his own resignation, and appealed to the Tsar to say that a Battenberg marriage into the royal family would endanger Russo–German relations. The Tsar, who did not want to embarrass Frederick, refused to say anything of the sort. Bismarck may have feared that Alexander was being groomed as his successor, and he also feared Franz von Roggenbach of Baden. The royal couple felt themselves so effectively cut off from trustworthy advisers that they were reduced to a secret correspondence with Ludwig Bamberger. After Frederick's death his son William, a brash young man who heartily shared Bismarck's anti-Liberal and anti-English sentiments, succeeded to the throne as the Emperor William II, and for at least a year he was willing to leave Bismarck in control. But they finally parted company in March 1890.

It would, however, be a misreading of Bismarck's record to suggest that the ultimate failure occurred only in his relations with the Hohenzollern family. A man of endless expedients, he had not exhausted the resources of opportunism by any means, but he was facing the breakdown, at home and abroad, of the whole political system that he had been constructing and defending since the seventies. We can understand his failure with William II only against the background of these broader issues, for although the young Emperor was undoubtedly looking for an excuse to assert himself he and his advisers were convinced (perhaps too easily, who can say), that they had solid grounds for a change of course.

Bismarck's own moves show only too clearly that he was aware of the virtual collapse of his diplomatic system in 1887. The essential feature of this had been the neutralization of French hostility by means of an entente or alliance with Russia and Austria. He had failed to convince the Russians in the seventies that he was a disinterested friend, but they had thought it worth while in 1881 to renew the alliance and to give him a free hand against France in order to prevent his quarrelsomeness from developing into open enmity. They hoped in return for advantages in the Balkans through his mediation or pressure on Austria. But by 1887 these hopes had been abandoned; they had refused to give him a free hand any longer against France, and had refused to commit themselves to any further collaboration with Austria. Apart from the reinsurance treaty, a mere marking of time, Bismarck's diplomatic arts had quite failed to manipulate Russian and Austrian policy according to his wishes. In response to mounting anti-German feeling in Russia he had indulged in some injudicious displays of retaliation (such as the war on Russian credit), while professing great concern to maintain the Tsar's goodwill (as in the Battenberg marriage question). The Russians, it is true, were exasperating neighbours. The fact remains that his Russian policy was in ruins by this stage.

So too was his French policy. He had neither crushed nor conciliated the French. His handling of the republic between 1871 and 1877 had made a war of revenge ultimately inevitable; his support of her colonial aims between 1878 and 1885 merely gave her colonies and some prestige without healing the breach. The events of 1886 and 1887 dispelled any lingering belief in Paris in his goodwill. But French self-confidence was growing, and in 1888 and 1889 it took the form of a fierce tariff war against Italy and such continued friction over Franco–Italian disputes in Africa as to raise the possibility of war. This sustained attack on the weakest member of the triple alliance worried Bismarck, but he could discover no means of restraining the French. Feeling more and more the need for a major reconstruction of his alliance system he played his last card—without success. Following a number of hints in 1888 he made a specific proposal to Salisbury for an Anglo–German alliance in January 1889, and on 26 January spoke of Britain in the Reichstag as an old and traditional ally, 'with whom we have no conflicting interests'. His suggestion was an alliance for one, two, or three years, which would be made public in order to have its maximum effect on the French. Salisbury, in spite of a very friendly response, rejected the plan in March, and his decision at the same time to strengthen the Royal Navy up to the Two-Power standard meant a choice for the risks of isolation rather than the embarrassing advantages of co-operation with Germany. For Bismarck this meant the final failure to construct an alliance system which would isolate the unforgiving French.

There was now little reality left in Bismarck's complicated alliance structure apart from the alliance with Austria, which held firm because it was based on his one unequivocal promise of support to an ally, and the alliance with Italy, a doubtful comfort. The real strength of Germany's position lay, we must say again, in Germany's own power, military and economic. Alliances or not, she was formidable; foreigners must take notice of her. For the rest, goodwill depended on her behaviour. The astonishing complexity of his arrangements could well lead an inexperienced ruler to feel that Bismarck and his team of experts were indispensable. But if the ruler were looking for grounds of dissent the very complexity could suggest an urgent need for simplification and a new vision.

It was in the domestic field, however, that Bismarck was to be openly defied by his new master. Here too he evidently hoped that his vast experience and command of all the machinery of government would make him indispensable. Yet during the winter of 1888–9 the Emperor was already showing, in his Chancellor's eyes, the faults of mercurial, callow, bumptious youth, and more specifically a cocksure belief in his own abilities and Germany's strength. The tendency to arrogance and personal offensiveness of the younger generation of officers and bureaucrats in Prussia was partly due to the fading away of the older sense of danger. Bismarck, who had terrified his seniors in the fifties with his bold plans, seemed now a monument of inhibitions, intolerable in his unanswerable arguments against change. But it had evidently not occurred to him that the Emperor would wish to challenge the basic assumptions on which the autocratic, monarchical system of government was based, and under which the Chancellor exercised power without being responsible to a cabinet or a party majority. He had broken with the National Liberals when they had tried in 1878 to graft a strengthened liberalism on their loyal nationalism. He continued to rely on the conservative parties, safely dug in in the Prussian Landtag through the restrictive franchise, and more precariously dominant in the Reichstag in the *Kartell*. If the Reichstag swung left in the next election he would manoeuvre, divide, and if necessary defy it, as in the past, relying on the Emperor's ultimate support. But William had quite different ideas. He would not defy but would capture the loyalty of the masses by a progressive social policy.

In Bismarck's eyes this meant surrender to the disruptive forces. His own repressive policy had been revealed in the anti-socialist legislation since 1878, and in his refusal to interfere between worker and employer in industrial disputes or by the introduction of any legislation to remove the obvious grievances of unsavoury factory conditions, excessive hours of labour, and the like. He took the line that he was maintaining the worker's natural right to work as long as he pleased, although he was quite prepared for the state to help in the social legislation which he introduced in the eighties and which left the freedom of employer and employee untouched. The Conservatives and Clericals had tried for some years after 1869 to secure a statutory limit of the working day, but Bismarck had defeated these attempts with the support of the Liberals, whose *Manchesterismus* was proof even against the arguments for factory inspection. From 1877 onwards the socialists pressed without success for a 10-hour working day. The first dramatic intervention by the young Emperor came in May 1889 during a serious strike among miners in the Ruhr. Having satisfied himself that they were living under atrocious conditions he appeared suddenly at a crown council, denounced the employers, and demanded immediate action; the miners did secure a favourable settlement shortly afterwards. After this he began to interest himself more and more in plans for factory reform and the protection of labour, while Bismarck was planning to take advantage of the *Kartell* majority to make the anti-socialist legislation permanent.

It has sometimes been argued that the Bismarck of the

sixties, who stuck closely to King William during the great crises, would not have left the young Emperor so much to his own devices. Bismarck's age and personality made it impossible for him to dance attendance on this young and volatile ruler, but he hoped that his son Herbert, who had certainly got on well with William in the past, would defend his father's interest. Herbert was aggressive and self-confident, without an ounce of his father's flair and sensitivity. William was listening to other advisers, including Count Waldersee, who was obsessed like Holstein with the danger from Russia and wanted a preventive war, and Professor Georg Hinzpeter, his former tutor, who encouraged him to think of his duty to his people. In October 1889, after the introduction of his new anti-socialist bill, Bismarck retired to Friedrichsruh to await developments. In long and confused debates the *Kartell* majority failed to agree among themselves about certain modifications in the clauses, and meanwhile the Emperor's advisers had drawn up a series of measures for the improvement of working class conditions. Bismarck was summoned back to Berlin peremptorily by the Kaiser on 23 January 1890; the anti-socialist bill was defeated on the 25th; and, in February, elections to the Reichstag took place which destroyed the *Kartell*, whose numbers dropped from 220 to 135. The opposition parties, the Radicals, Social Democrats, and the Centre, worked together and now dominated the Reichstag with a decisive majority. It was the end of the Bismarckian system as Germany had known it since 1871.

It was this new situation that led Bismarck and the Emperor almost immediately to their final breach. William was not pleased with the position, for he wanted support for a new army bill. But he hoped to make a good impression with the labour legislation, whereas Bismarck wished to carry things through with a high hand, resisting concessions to the Left, and if necessary staging a *coup d'état* with a revised constitution. He tried to secure an alliance with the Centre, but Windthorst was amused and

unco-operative. William accepted Bismarck's resignation
on 20 March 1890. Bismarck did his best to make the immediate cause of dispute a demand by the Emperor for the
repeal of Manteuffel's Order of 1852, which required
the minister-president's authorization of contacts between
the King of Prussia and his ministers; this suggested
that the Emperor wished to be his own chancellor. However, the issues were wider than that; wider even than the
decision as to whether the Bismarck dynasty or the Hohenzollern dynasty should reign. Germany, and not merely
the young Emperor, was at last ready to drop the pilot.

Bismarck's last years were spent in a rather embittered
retirement. In 1891 he was elected a member of the
Reichstag, but never took his seat. He meant to write his
memoirs, and instead kept drifting off into long reminis-
cences about the past, to the neglect of any systematic
writing. The faithful Lothar Bucher tried to bring some
shape and accuracy to the story until his death in 1892.
Moritz Busch and Herbert Bismarck gave some help.
They were published after his death—a collection of brilliant set pieces and reflexions, but not a continuous story.
His wife died in 1894. He talked a good deal at first about
a return to power, and it could not be denied that his successors looked humdrum and quite lacking in genius;
yet no one seriously wanted him back. Hohenlohe noted
the almost universal feeling of relief on his departure.
'Each separate personality is now conscious of his own
value', he wrote on 18 June 1890. 'Formerly the individual was oppressed and restricted by the dominant influence of Prince Bismarck, but now they have all swelled
out like sponges placed in water.' This was true not only
of officials in their personal careers, but more generally
of the country and its leaders; the urge to expand, satisfied for awhile in the seventies but growing ever more insistent throughout the eighties, now found expression in a
dynamic policy, or a whole range of dynamic policies,
which were often disconcerting to Germany's neighbours
and a fundamental rejection of the limited objectives of

the Bismarck era. The old man was critical, alarmed, and at times vindictive in carefully planned indiscretions.

There were some perfunctory gestures of reconciliation on the part of the Emperor, and the German people knew that the great Chancellor was one of the immortals, even if the Reichstag refused to celebrate his eightieth birthday. Lonely, rather neglected by his family, nursing all his hates and resentments, he died on 30 July 1898, at the age of 83.

Chapter Seven

Modern Germany and Bismarck

BISMARCK'S reputation at the time of his retirement was based partly on achievement, partly on endurance. The achievements which astonished the world and which continue to be viewed with a deep satisfaction by nearly all his countrymen are those of his first period, down to 1871. They were essentially and almost exclusively political. The soldiers won the wars; the peasants and factory hands, the steelmasters and landlords, the bankers and entrepreneurs, made the economy powerful; what Germany had to offer the world in culture owed little to his inspiration. But Germany, the land of immemorial disunity, had been pushed, cajoled, disciplined, and manoeuvred into greatness by one man, and the means could be comfortably defended as both brilliant and praiseworthy.

After 1871 the achievement was of a somewhat different character. Bismarck survived, and so did the empire. It was therefore not an ephemeral structure, as Napoleon III's had been. He gained new credit as the defender and developer of his own solid work. On the other hand the nineteen years of peace, and the normal secrecy of international diplomacy, concealed from the German people many of the shifts and embarrassments of his foreign policy, although the shrill and venomous exchanges of German domestic politics were well enough known. On balance the picture that finally emerged was a somewhat idealized one of a Germanic superman, majestic and old and terrible and all-wise. As Erich Marcks, the most graceful of his German biographers, told an English audience in 1902, he was

... a ruler of the great Germanic type, lion-like in temperament as in the glance of his powerful eyes; dangerous to enemies and allies, demoniacally defiant in his strength, crushing, pitiless. And yet bending—autocratic and reckless as he was in his choice of practical means—yet bending in the service of general forces : full of a deep faith till the end, supported by his religion, though his was not a religion of mildness and 'love your enemies'.

Thus the long years of peaceful rule and political survival after 1870 reinforced the assumption of his complete mastery of all situations, and the Bismarck legend—essentially a legend of infallibility—was born.

Marcks had no doubt as to the nature of Germany's debt to Bismarck. 'He educated us', he said on the same occasion.

He urged men perhaps too exclusively to power, work, and practical issues; well, these shortcomings have since then corrected themselves in the natural course of time; but what he is to us, what he gave and gives us, that remains indispensable to us; he made us strong and manly.

This was a typical national-liberal judgment, giving thanks for the national achievement and condoning the 'shortcomings'. The cult of the strong and manly led, however, to disasters in two world wars, and finally—but only in recent years—German voices have begun to ask whether they had after all been taught the right lessons, or whether they had perhaps misunderstood the teaching of the master.

Accordingly the criticism or appraisal of Bismarck's work has tended to be on two levels. There was first a vast body of writing, mainly eulogistic, by those who were interested in his political and diplomatic technique, and who wanted to discover and expound the secrets of his success, or simply to demonstrate their own acuteness in explaining his subtle moves. There was secondly the

writing of those who asked in more general terms whether
the purpose, example, and influence of his multitudinous
activities were beneficial to Germany or to mankind, in
accordance with whatever standards of judgment the
author had set himself. Ideally, biographers should work
simultaneously at both levels, for each is essential to the
understanding of the other. Generalizations about Bismarck's aims and purpose can easily go wrong unless they
are developed with a full knowledge of his actual per-
formances. On the other hand the understanding of his
detailed moves can easily be marred by a failure to relate
them to his general outlook and deeply-rooted prejudices
and loyalties.

Instead, what happened during the two generations
after Bismarck's death was that full-length biographies
appeared rather infrequently, and there was a spate of
books, articles, doctoral dissertations and the like dealing
in great detail with short phases and isolated problems
of his career. This was particularly true during the inter-
war period, after the publication of six volumes of German diplomatic correspondence in 1922 covering the
seventies and eighties. Much of this writing, in spite of
its careful study of the documents, is unsatisfactory because of the assumption of deep plots, long-term policies,
subtle manoeuvres on the part of the 'greatest diplomatist
of modern times', which exist only in the imagination of
the authors. Thus the American historian, J. V. Fuller, to
give one example, saw in the events of 1887 an elaborate
plan to solve the Near Eastern question in Austria's
interest and to expel the Russians 'once and for all' from
the Balkans.

There is some indication that this tendency was encouraged by the German Foreign Office, for the six
volumes of documents have since been found to be highly
selective; it seems that the editors simply did not print
documents which conflicted with the standardized picture
of a peace-loving diplomatic genius in action. Many key
documents dealing with the Hohenzollern candidature
were also withheld. German, American, and British his-

torians who wanted to believe that Bismarck was a lover of peace because they wanted peace to prevail in their own age were thus tempted to idealize the ironical chancellor, who would have been amused at their conclusions. In general, then, much of this writing is vitiated by partly false assumptions, such as that Bismarck's broader decisions and judgments were always right, that the documentation is complete, that Germany's failures were due essentially to his successors, and that the more one talked about Bismarck the peacemaker the more likely was peace to be preserved in one's own lifetime. It was, however, Bismarck the pacemaker of the first decade who dominated the minds of Germany's leaders. It was the man who made successful war by isolating his enemies. In mid-July 1914 the younger (and lesser) von Moltke pondered the adroit moves whereby Bismarck struck down Austria without foreign interference in 1866. Hitler, in March 1938, on the eve of his Austrian coup, recalled Bismarck's clever diplomacy against the French in 1870.

Bismarck, the violent, cunning, power-mad, patriotic Junker, an interesting man whatever else one could say about him, was in danger of becoming sanctified out of existence by his scholarly admirers. The fact is that the political development of Germany for a long time made criticism of his record somewhat distasteful. The first phase of contemporary or near-contemporary writing about him came mainly from German National-Liberal circles to whom his achievements seemed indisputable, and his abilities obviously superior to those of the young Kaiser and his advisers. They felt that they had been made strong and manly, but they had also been given peace and the *Rechtsstaat*, unity and parliamentary government. Sybel and Treitschke among German historians were contemporaries who had been converted by his success in 1866; the two considerable biographers of the early 20th century, Erich Marcks and Max Lenz, were also admirers, although they were scholarly in their presentation of the facts, as they understood them. William II, who resented Bismarck's fame, was gratified by Ottokar Lorenz's life of the Emperor William I, published in 1902; but this attempt to upset Sybel's interpretation and present the old Kaiser as the real creator of the empire convinced no one.

Germany's defeat in 1918 and the Social-Democratic repudiation of the past which led to the Weimar constitution might have been expected to produce a revaluation of Bismarck's methods and aims. There was some attempt in Germany and abroad to place responsibility for Germany's disasters on Bismarck's shoulders. Spengler has some comments on these lines, and at Göttingen during the twenties Professor Max Lehmann criticized Bismarck's machiavellianism and betrayal of Liberalism in domestic politics. But these lines of criticism were soon swamped by the psychological need of the new Germany for a folk-hero, as an assurance of the possibility of future greatness. The more unsparingly the Kaiser's Germany was condemned, the more urgent became the need for proof that, under proper leadership, Germany could be great again. Hitler it is true accepted the Bismarck legend a little coolly; he was apparently not disposed to praise so recent a predecessor too highly, and Nazi propagandists preferred to hero-worship Frederick the Great.

The gloom and despair which overwhelmed Germans after the second world war produced not so much a repudiation of the past as a conviction that the end had come—the end, that is, of the Europe which they knew and to which both the second and the third Reich belonged. In 1945 Albert Weber saw in the blindness and frivolity of those who had unleashed modern war on a shrunken world the end of the 'old history', as he put it, inaugurated by the equestrian tribes 1,200 years before Christ. 'Girt round with demons, a hand over one eye but staring with the other into horrors, she plunges from despair to deeper despair', wrote Thomas Mann in 1947. Perhaps it was typical of German pessimism that the end of a phase of German predominance should be equated with the end of Europe, and a recovery from these extremes of gloom soon began. Nevertheless, the way lay forward to the economic miracle and the Western Germany of Adenauer and the Atlantic Community, rather than back by whatever devious and disguised courses to the Bismarckian Reich. Hitler's work could now be heartily repudiated : it was the eruption of the satanic principle in world history, and a great many other things too. But this view led, as Friedrich Meinecke pointed out in 1946, to an obvious query which could not be shirked : 'whether the germs of the later evil were not really implanted in Bismarck's work from the outset'.

This quotation from Meinecke's essay on *The German Catastrophe*, published first in German and later in an English translation, may be said to have inaugurated a searching reassessment of Bismarck's career, mainly on the second level mentioned above. The comments of the greatest of living German historians were far different from those of A. O. Meyer, whose long and respectful biography of Bismarck, finished in 1943 and published in 1949, was in the older tradition. Meinecke recognized that Bismarck's Empire gave too much play to Prussian militarism and with it to the dangerous mentality of Prussian self-sufficiency 'which it could create or foster in the Empire's leaders and in the bourgeoisie'. Of course, this had been a truism in the 'blood and iron' school of foreign criticism ever since the eighteen-sixties, but it was a new note indeed in German historiography. Even now the octogenarian Meinecke looked back on his enthusiastic reception of Bismarck's achievement in founding the empire as 'a precious memory'. 'We Germans often felt so free and proud, in contrast with the whole previous German past, in the mightily flourishing Empire of 1871 which gave living space to every one of us !' It was simply that, dazzled by the brilliance, they 'saw too little the hidden, dark points' where the empire was vulnerable to disease. The popularity of the anti-Semitic rector Ahlwardt in the early eighties might now, for example, be seen as a prelude to Hitler's later success; but the suggestion would have been laughed at at the time. The Germans had felt secure under the reign of law.

Meinecke in fact had largely begged the question of Bismarck's personal responsibility for the later disasters : he did not seem to think that Bismarck was himself aware of the 'dark spots', or that he would have allowed them to develop, or even that he was responsible for their existence. The old man's nostalgic memories of the happy, splendid dawn of the empire could hardly be shared by his younger contemporaries among the historians, and in the new political and social world of the nineteen-fifties Bismarck did at last fade from the popular consciousness into a chapter of history—for those who still read any history.* Among historians, however, the debate continued, moving on balance in Bismarck's favour. The essential point in dispute was, however, still the one which Meinecke had raised, and which tended to produce wide but inconclusive discussion. On the whole, although with some notable exceptions, German historians deny that Hitlerism was a necessary development of Bismarckism, and can quote in support Bismarck's circumspect use of force, his opposition to preventive wars, his religious faith, his indifference to *grossdeutsch* or pangerman ambitions, his satisfaction after 1870 with Germany's place in a European balance of power, and his determination to maintain the supremacy of the political over the military authority. While there have been some able critics of these views, there is general agreement as to Bismarck's essentially opportunistic approach to nationalism. As Professor Gerhart Ritter remarked in his important work, *Europa und die Deutsche Frage*, in 1948, he was unmoved by the fanaticism of modern nationalist movements. Writers like A. O. Meyer, who tended to think of the story in terms of a triumphant crusade for national unification, were no longer taken very seriously.

* It was reported in 1956 that in a general knowledge test the Cologne Chamber of Commerce had recently asked about 1,750 German apprentices who Bismarck was. Rather more than one-third thought he was either a herring, the Emperor of Austria, or a shipbuilder. On the other hand every apprentice correctly identified 19 different makes of car.

What emerges clearly from the writings of Germany's recent historians is an almost universal acceptance of the geopolitical character of the German state in the form given it by Bismarck. We cannot doubt that in this matter the historical sense is reinforced by loyalty to the Germanic political tradition which finds a transitory expression in the Bonn regime. The only alternative to the Bismarckian Reich to receive any consideration has been Constantin Frantz's contemporary sketch of a federated central Europe. This found an advocate in Professor Franz Schnabel, whose views, however, have aroused little enthusiasm. Nor have those of Bismarck's most formidable critic, the late Dr. Erich Eyck, a refugee from Nazi Germany, whose three-volume biography, published in Switzerland between 1941 and 1944, was a survey of Bismarck's whole life and career from the viewpoint of a *deutsch-freisinniger*, or even a Gladstonian, Liberal. But Eyck like the others accepted the Bismarckian Reich as a necessary and legitimate satisfaction of German needs. The rather impatient rejection in Germany of Eyck's interpretation is as much a rejection of 19th century Liberalism as a refusal to recognize the cumulative effect of his formidable criticism of many facets of Bismarck's career.

In the present short study the attempt has been made to examine Bismarck's handling of policy in its contemporary setting, avoiding as far as possible the many acute controversies that accompanied and followed his stormy progress. One particular point which emerges from such a study is the extent to which events and conditions in Germany and Prussia dictated his course; if Bismarck made modern Germany, modern Germany made Bismarck, and not only in the sense that it established his fame. It is certainly quite misleading to speak of him as the sole architect and mechanic of German fortunes or misfortunes, as if Germany consisted of docile and inanimate material that could be shaped exclusively by one man.

Bismarck did not come into politics with ready-made

plans or unswerving principles which he proceeded to force down the throats of his neighbours during the next forty years. It is true that he enjoyed the role of the intransigent young diehard and Junker trouble-shooter during the revolutionary years, but he was finding his feet for the first time in politics, and the role was ready-made and well suited to his early contacts and prejudices. Very soon in the Frankfurt period however his desire to conquer power and an impatient awareness of the need to manipulate man and interests made him a conscious *Realpolitiker* and improviser, and from this time until his final retirement there seemed to be hardly any policy, alliance, or individual which might not be sacrificed to suit his purpose. Similarly his willingness to adapt policy endlessly to the conquest of power (for himself and the state) involved a wide measure of accommodation to interests for which he had in many cases no spontaneous sympathy. In these matters he was no different from successful politicians in all times and countries. The only office which could provide full satisfaction of his personal ambition was that of minister-president of Prussia, and political survival, as much as the urge to dazzle the world with his achievements, drove him along the path which ended at Versailles in 1871.

At every turn of his career he was the agent and exploiter of forces and policies which he was later believed, in the days of his towering eminence, to have created. A moment's thought will show the absurdity of saying, for example, that Bismarck or even 'the Bismarckian system' created Prussian militarism. Dr. Otto Pflanze, in his recent authoritative study of Bismarck's early career, goes so far as to assert that all the unique features in Germany's development were in existence long before Bismarck's day. He finds their origin in the peculiar linking of the Prussian political, social, and military systems, the late appearance of a German middle class, the Lutheran subjection of church to state, the victory of historical over natural law, the idealization of the state and its power, and the acceptance of culture rather than citizenship as the basis of the German view of nationality. When Bismarck came to office the prestige of the Prussian officer class over all other public servants was well established, the army was possibly strong enough already to fight Austria or France successfully, and the military cabinet had almost succeeded in freeing itself of all political control. The four years of the constitutional struggle were as much a means of preventing the complete dominance of King William by the army leaders as of preventing the weakening of the army by the Landtag. Bismarck had to associate with them and satisfy them in order to keep some hold over them, and he was seldom seen in public without his general's uniform after 1866. He said that the high collar kept his neck warm.

In the same way his attitude towards German nationalism is very much that of the practical politician making do with whatever will serve his purpose. Historians have spent much time in arguing as to the character of the nationalistic elements in Bismarck's policy of unification. Was he from the start, or did he become at a certain date, a 'German' as distinct from a 'Prussian' patriot? We certainly find him saying as early as April 1849, 'who speaks German wants German unity'—lip service at least to cultural nationalism—but ten years later he seemed to be thinking in terms of an expanded Prussia when he pondered the use of the *Zollverein* system for this purpose. If by nationalism we mean emotional support and crusading zeal for the somewhat nebulous political entity called Germany, as it was visualized for example by the leaders in the Frankfurt parliament, then it is certain that Bismarck was not a German nationalist. On the other hand the practical advantages of a new political creation which could be called Germany and which would include some or all of the remaining German states with Prussia in the dominant position were very much in his thoughts from 1849 onwards. Bismarck was thus a man of great political ability who down to 1871 did his work and used the material at hand more successfully than any of his contemporaries could have done, but what he did was

what his Prussian contemporaries—almost but not quite
to a man—desired. If there is anything reprehensible in
the German outlook or use of power they must share it
with him. His progress was conditioned by the capacities,
frustrations, latent resources and conflicting ambitions of
the Germany and Europe of his day; although to preserve a sense of proportion we must remember that his
admirers often exaggerate the extent of the obstacles in
his path. In the Weimar period, when the world seemed
so hostile, German historians tended to assume that it had
been the same in the sixties, although in fact Bismarck's
opponents had a remarkable knack of isolating themselves.

His dependence on circumstance is further emphasized
by the frustrations that dogged him so frequently in the
period after 1871. It was less successful than the first
period, in spite of the fact that his power and authority
had not weakened; his peculiar political gifts and exper-
tise were indeed at their height. But German conditions
in both the foreign and domestic fields were less able to
provide him with the type of triumph that he had enjoyed
before. We may well ask whether the mere feat of endurance—the nineteen years of office after 1871—has not
led everyone to exaggerate the extent of his later achievements. He stayed in office because three emperors kept
him there, not because he consistently won fresh triumphs
or consistently pleased a majority of the electorate.

Deprived by his own free will of the opportunity to
consummate short phases of provocative policy with a
swift and crushing use of force he never learned how to
carry out the alternative, that of peaceful collaboration,
convincingly. This is true of both his domestic and foreign
policy after 1871. His suspicions and combative outlook
made it impossible for him to form relations of enduring
trust with party leaders at home or politicians abroad,
just as he had no friends in private life after those of his
youth dropped out one by one through age or death. He
came nearest to a full political alliance in his co-operation
with the Liberals in the seventies, but broke with them

when they wanted a Liberal cabinet, and always opposed some aspects of their programme. The Conservatives took their place in large measure in the eighties, but were less demanding. He talked continually of the domestic *Reichsfeinde* and conducted his violent campaigns against the Catholics in the seventies and socialists in the eighties, obviously feeling that his creation was beset with dangers, although this assumption that the enemies were gathering around him was largely a myth. In some future generation the French might resume the fight, but otherwise Europe was only too willing to let the new Germany alone, if it could prove that it was indeed a satiated state. Nor were the domestic enemies any more than interest groups out to get the best for themselves within the framework of the state.

Moved by this oppressive sense of danger, his political methods also gradually changed; whereas before 1871 he was adept at pursuing alternative policies up to the critical moment for decisive action, he later practised more and more the policy of alternating severity with concessions as a means of commanding support. It was not particularly successful; the social security legislation for example did not attract the working-class voters who knew all about the anti-socialist laws, and, if they were Catholic, the May laws. In foreign affairs the policy of alternating rewards and recriminations might be said to have succeeded in the case of Austria, for she alone received something tangible, in the shape of a promise of military support, to balance former blows. Russia, France, and Great Britain could only regard him as an incalculable neighbour who would give nothing away but with whom it was best to avoid an open quarrel if possible. In a curious way his policy of peace and consolidation seemed to keep Europe and his own regime in the constant state of suspense and impending crisis which it must be presumed he genuinely wished to avoid.

His greatest failure lay in his inability to develop among the diverse political elements of the new Germany a politically responsible class and a workable system of responsible government. This need not necessarily have been on the western parliamentary model. Within the framework of the new Reich particularism had taken new forms : the older political isolationism of the states had been succeeded by the self-centred dynamism of powerful interest-groups, ranging from the great business combines, the General Staff, and the Junker agrarians to class and confessional parties, large and small. The concentration of ultimate power in himself and the Emperor, in what was essentially an irresponsible regime, had not only the more obvious weakness of a failure to provide an adequate successor to himself. It also meant that his own masterly rule could never be more than a successful balancing, diverting, and thwarting of the ambitions of other men. Although these men were no doubt patriotic Germans in spirit they had not been accustomed through their leaders to long familiarity with the general interests and the practical, day-to-day administrative difficulties of the state. Parliamentarism, which Bismarck sometimes equated with Revolution, thus served only to voice demands and train critics, and to confirm his pessimistic views about the inadequacy of all alternatives to himself.

Disraeli, who put Bismarck in his last novel, *Endymion*, slightly disguised as the Count of Ferroll, advised his readers to suspend judgment. 'He is a man neither to love nor to detest. He has himself an intelligence superior to all passion, I might say all feeling; and if, in dealing with such a person, we ourselves have either, we might give him an advantage.' But to a later age Bismarck does not appear as a man superior to all passion, and perhaps he was more handicapped by it than his opponents. The sense of relief at his dismissal and the temporary reassertion of the individual will that accompanied it, meant for a moment the ending of his struggle against immemorial disunity. We must regard the hatreds, the overwrought nerves, the distortion of perspective that disfigured his later career as the overstrain of a thirty-years' campaign in which his genius had gained exaggerated value in his own eyes as the rallying point of a new national life.

Note on Books

Bismarck wrote enormously, and very well. His private letters, official papers and correspondence, speeches, table talk and memoirs have been published copiously but not completely. A great collected edition, reprinting many earlier collections with corrections and additions and including much new material, was undertaken during the inter-war years, under various editors. This is :

> *Bismarck: die gesammelten Werke* (Friedrichsruher Ausgabe, ed. Thimme, Andreas, and others, 1923 onwards).

It includes a large part of his official correspondence before he became minister-president in 1862. Much of his subsequent official diplomatic correspondence is contained in two famous series :

> *Die Auswärtige Politik Preussens, 1858–1871* (1930 onwards, published by the German Historische Reichskommission).
> *Die Grosse Politik der europäischen Kabinette, 1871–1914* (published for the German foreign office : the first six volumes cover the period 1871–1890 (1922).

However, the full correspondence in the archives of the German foreign office, which is now available to students in Bonn, and in microfilm in the Public Record Office in London and elsewhere, contains much additional material which may necessitate major revisions of Bismarck's record. A good example of the importance of this unpublished material was shown by the following, a collection of documents which gave for the first time the inside story of Bismarck's part in the Hohenzollern candidature from February to July 1870 :

> Georges Bonnin (ed.), *Bismarck and the Hohenzollern Candidature for the Spanish Throne* (London, 1957).

There were a number of biographies of Bismarck soon after his death; of these the best in English was that by C. Grant Robertson (1918). But these works were to some extent put out of date by the new documentary material which appeared from 1919 onwards, and historians for the next twenty years or so confined themselves to writing studies of special aspects and incidents of his career, mainly in the post-1870 diplomatic field. Then after 1940 a new series of substantial biographies, which had assimilated the more specialized studies and new material, began to appear. They included :

> Erich Eyck, *Bismarck, Leben und Werk* (Zurich, 3 vols, 1941, 1943, 1944).
>
> A. O. Meyer, *Bismarck, Der Mensch und der Staatsmann* (Stuttgart, 1949).
>
> L. Reimers, *Bismarck* (Munich, 2 vols, 1956–7).
>
> W. Mommsen, *Bismarck, Ein politisches Lebensbild* (Munich, 1959).
>
> O. Pflanze, *Bismarck and the Development of Germany: The Period of Unification, 1815–1871* (Princeton, 1963, the first of two volumes).

Meyer and Reimers are admirers of Bismarck; the others more critical. Professor Pflanze's work promises to become the major authority for English readers, for whom two shorter biographies are available by Erich Eyck (London, 1950, an abridgement of his longer work), and by A. J. P. Taylor (London, 1955). The following may be mentioned among the numerous studies of aspects of Bismarck's personality and domestic policy :

> O. Becker, *Bismarcks Ringen um Deutschlands Gestaltung* (Heidelberg, 1958).

G. A. Craig, *The Politics of the Prussian Army, 1640–1945* (Oxford, 1955).

W. H. Dawson, *Social Insurance in Germany, 1883–1911* (London, 1912).

G. Goyau, *Bismarck et l'église* (Paris, 1911–13).

T. S. Hamerow, *Restoration, Revolution, Reaction, Economics and Politics in Germany, 1815–1871* (Princeton, 1958).

W. Mommsen, *Bismarcks Stutz und die Parteien* (Berlin, 1924).

The following works deal in the main with Bismarck's diplomacy and external policy :

C. W. Clark, *Franz Joseph and Bismarck* (Harvard, 1934).

S. E. Crowe, *The Berlin West African Conference* (London, 1942).

F. Haselmayr, *Diplomatische Geschichte des Zweiten Reichs von 1871–1918* (Munich, vol. 1).

W. N. Medlicott, *Bismarck, Gladstone, and the Concert of Europe* (London, 1957).

B. Nolde, *Die Petersburger Mission Bismarcks, 1859–1862* (Leipzig, 1936).

H. Rothfels, *Bismarcks englische Bündnispolitik* (Berlin, 1924).

L. D. Steefel, *The Schleswig-Holstein Question* (Harvard, 1932).

L. D. Steefel, *Bismarck, the Hohenzollern Candidacy, and the Origins of the Franco–German War of 1870* (Harvard, 1962).

M. E. Townshend, *The Rise and Fall of Germany's Colonial Empire 1884–1918* (New York, 1930).

W. Windelband, *Bismarck und die europäischen Grossmächte, 1879–1885* (Essen, 1942).

There are convenient discussions of the 'Bismarck problem' in the first chapter of Pflanze's work, mentioned above, and in 'The Study of Bismarck' by G. P. Gooch (in his *Studies in German History*, London, 1948). F.

Meinecke, in *The German Catastrophe* (Harvard, 1950), gives a critical view of some of the consequences of Bismarck's career for Germany. This theme is developed in *German History, some new German Views* (London, 1954), a valuable collection of essays edited by Dr. Hans Kohn.

Index

73 74   12 11 10 9 8 7 6 5